Pārvatīdarpaṇa

Pārvatīdarpaṇa

An exposition of Kāśmīr Śaivism through the images of Śiva and Pārvatī

(Second Edition with 16 Colour Plates)

Harsha V. Dehejia

MOTILAL BANARSIDASS PUBLISHERS
PRIVATE LIMITED • DELHI

*Second Edition : Delhi, **2010***
First Edition : Delhi, 2008

ISBN : 978-81-208-1483-7 (Cloth)
ISBN : 978-81-208-1484-4 (Paper)

MOTILAL BANARSIDASS
41 U.A. Bungalow Road, Jawahar Nagar, Delhi 110 007
8 Mahalaxmi Chamber, 22 Bhulabhai Desai Road, Mumbai 400 026
203 Royapettah High Road, Mylapore, Chennai 600 004
236, 9th Main III Block, Jayanagar, Bangalore 560 011
Sanas Plaza, 1302 Baji Rao Road, Pune 411 002
8 Camac Street, Kolkata 700 017
Ashok Rajpath, Patna 800 004
Chowk, Varanasi 221 001

PRINTED IN INDIA
By Jainendra Prakash Jain at Shri Jainendra Press,
A-45, Naraina, Phase-I, New Delhi 110 028
and Published by Narendra Prakash Jain for
Motilal Banarsidass Publishers Private Limited,
Bungalow Road, Delhi 110 007

Dedicated to Sudha
who, by the way she lives
has taught me the meaning of *śraddhā*
and to Vivek and Rajeev
who, by what they stand for
have defined intellectuality for me.

Contents

Foreword

The glory of Hindu philosophy lies in its many-splendoured and multiple approaches to the Divine. Hinduism is the only religion in the world not based upon the teachings of a single individual or text, which means that it is not pegged to any rigid formulation of the spiritual path, but rather represents the collective wisdom of seers and sages down from the Vedic age, at least five thousand years ago, to our own day. Hinduism thus provides a unique spectrum of approaches to spiritual striving and aspiration.

Some schools of thought posit an Absolute which is beyond name and form, Śaṅkara's *advaita* being the most powerful exposition of this path. However, there is a profusion of other brilliant expositions by great Ācāryas or teachers such as Rāmānuja, Madhva, Vallabha and Abhinavagupta; the latter, the greatest exponent of what has come to be known as Kāśmīr Śaivism. This creative reinterpretation of the eternal truths embodied in the Vedas and Upaniṣads continues down to our own century when spiritual giants like Swāmī Vivekānanda, Śrī Raman Maharṣi and Śrī Aurobindo made their unique contribution to the unfolding panorama of Hindu philosophy.

It is important to understand that Indian philosophy is not merely an intellectual gymnastic, but revolves around a cluster of intellectual, physical and spiritual disciplines which should lead to a sharpening and clarifying of consciousness and, finally, to spiritual realisation. The Sanskrit word for philosophy is *darśana*, which means 'to see', not merely to think or to ratiocinate. Indeed, philosophy devoid of spiritual content, is looked upon in the entire Eastern tradition as a dry and ultimately sterile intellectualism.

Kāśmīr Śaivism can be described as the most prominent system in what is known as the Tāntric tradition. *Tantra*, which is in some ways a progression from *vedāntic* thinking, involves not a negation of life, but rather a positive life-affirmation, seeking to promote a set of values which are ethically good as well as pleasant to the individual. The long and interesting history of *Tantra* shows that while it is based upon Vedic foundations, it has incorporated a number of other lesser known but extremely virile traditions, which over the centuries, developed in various parts of India and Nepal. The central concept of Kāśmīr Śaivism is that Śiva is not only the creator of the universe but also permeates its every atom, so that the world is not to be wished away as an illusion but cherished as the voluntary manifestation of the power and glory of the divine. The formless, blissful Śiva, becoming the universe, involves what is known as *spanda* or vibration, which is why Kāśmīr Śaivism is also called *Spandaśāstra*.

The first significant series of texts and studies on Kāśmīr Śaivism were brought out during my father's reign in the late 1920s and early 1930s. It is now heartening to see a renewed interest by modern scholars in this fascinating school of Hindu philosophy. The present work by Dr. Harsha V. Dehejia approaches the basic tenets of Kāśmīr Śaivism through the central myth of the marriage of Śiva and Pārvatī, representing the union of the blissful, formless spirit with the dynamic energy that permeates the universe. This is a myth full of symbolic significance, and is reflected throughout the Hindu tradition in various forms—literary as well as iconographical. The famous Madurai sculpture of Viṣṇu giving Pārvatī's hand in marriage to Śiva is a classic example of this, as also the shrine of Śuddha Mahādeva near Jammu where, according to legend, the marriage actually took place.

The author has chosen the astonishing iconographical image of Ardhanārīśvara, Śiva and Pārvatī united in a single figure — half male and half female, to illustrate the inner significance of the myth, and has also, in an act of bold philosophical imagination, used this image to highlight the basic tenets of Kāśmīr Śaivism, and has brought home the fact that this is often referred to as the Yoga of delight or the Yoga of art, and involves a transmutation of consciousness, not by a process of negation, but by a joyous affirmation. He has focused our attention upon the mirror in Pārvatī's hand in which, seeing his own consciousness reflected, Śiva attains integrality, which then results in the creation and sustenance of what the Upaniṣads call 'this magnificent universe'.

An even more dramatic symbol is the glorious iconography of Śiva Naṭarāja, Lord of the cosmic Dance, a syncretic image which includes creation (the drum), destruction (the fire), preservation (the upraised hand) and the liberating wisdom (represented by the fourth hand pointing to his raised foot). Here again the creative symbiotic duality between the male and female elements are symbolized by the fact, that in one ear Naṭarāja wears a male earring and in the other a female one. Perhaps in his next book Dr. Dehejia could use this great figure to further exposit the joyous and life affirming philosophy of Kāśmīr Śaivism. Meanwhile, I have pleasure in commending ***Pārvatīdarpaṇa,*** to all those who are interested in Hindu philosophy and its creative interpretations.

KARAN SINGH

Chapter 1

Prologue

India reveals itself to me through images rather than through ideology, through gestures rather than through words and through myth rather than through history. While accepting the grandeur of the *nirguṇa brahman* I have been consistently drawn to the beauty of the *saguṇa brahman*, a *brahman* that I come to love and know through music and movement, through the creations of the potter and the poet. The Indian tradition has been called a palimpsest where a system of thought comes into being, becomes the dominant mode of thought and defines that period of civilisation for a few centuries and then mysteriously disappears, but not completely. Like the faded writing on the palimpsest it remains in the background, while another stream of thought arises and takes dominance over the minds of the people. These interruptions in the tradition have always intrigued me and made me wonder what it was that led to the weakening of what was once almost impregnable and, more importantly, what keeps the tradition going in an almost unbroken stream. Thus the Indus Valley Civilisation gave way to the Vedas the Vedas gave way to the Upaniṣads and with it *yajña* was transformed into *tapas*. And then a Hindu comes along and touches the people with his ideas of *karuṇā* and *nirvāṇa* and in a few centuries the entire continent becomes Buddhist. And when it appeared that all of India was turning to the Buddha, Hinduism springs back but in a different form and the *bhakti* cult takes hold of the people. Scholars have offered explanations why a certain system of thought weakens. It has been suggested that the Indus Valley Civilisation perished because of a natural disaster such as flood or because of the more mobile and aggressive Āryan civilisation. However it has never been adequately explained what hidden springs of strength keep the tradition alive and bring it back albeit in a transformed form. For, it is these springs that have sustained the tradition and ensured that despite the changes the underlying spirit remains the same. And at every turning point it is these ancient springs that have fed the river of Indian civilisation and kept it flowing. While pondering over the river of Indian civilisation it has occurred to me that it is the pre-historic folk tradition that has been its spring, its source of sustenance, its backbone. It is from this folk tradition that the ideas and images have arisen, it is the autochthonous people that have kept the ancient stories alive and passed them on from generation to generation, it is from their simple folklore that classical ideas have emerged, it is the earth that has nourished the seeds that have grown into majestic *nyagrodha* trees, it is the common people of the Indian soil, who love telling and listening to stories, who have been the repository of not only practical wisdom but equally of knowledge. It is therefore fitting that in expositing the epistemology of a major school of Indian thought I turn to an ancient myth. An epistemology can be exposited didactically and intramurally, and this is the accepted method in philosophical discourse, but using an ancient myth to elucidate an epistemology, is like illustrating an idea through a story rather than elucidating it through dicta, for a story like an image can incorporate a thousand words. A story and especially a mythic story, breaks away from arid discourse, but the discerning storyteller and listener alike are never unaware of seminal hints contained within the story. A story, and a mythic story in particular, therefore, is never just a narrative but contains within it layers and nuances of meanings. Were it not for this, the *krīḍā* of *nāṭya* would not have been fit for the *devas* and the *Nāṭyaśāstra* would not have been called the fifth Veda.

Scholars have written extensively on various schools of philosophy. There are erudite interpretations, scholarly commentaries and intellectual exegesis. But the erudition and scholarship seem arid and unimaginative. The folk tradition has been largely an oral tradition, spontaneously joyous and celebratory. The exposition that follows is that of a Śiva *rasika* who is not a mere voyeur at his romantic alliance with Pārvatī but delighting in the many moods of Śiva.

Chapter 2

The Spirit of the Āgamas

The Indian tradition is neither unitarian nor monolithic and one discovers a large number of views about matters finite and infinite, the apparent and the real and about immediate and ultimate reality. It is not useful to engage in a discussion that raises hierarchical questions about these varied schools of philosophy or their scriptures, nor is it useful to probe historical or anthropological questions surrounding these schools. Such an exercise proves futile to a large extent. Some Western interpreters of the Indian tradition have tried to do this and this has often resulted in many erroneous observations regarding the tradition. For instance the European view of the Āryan migration into the Indian subcontinent is being seriously questioned by present-day Indologists. The dominance of the classical system of thought, likewise, is being challenged by subaltern ideologies even within the tradition.

It is customary to divide the main scriptures of the Indian tradition into four groups: Vedas, Smṛtis, Purāṇas and the Āgamas. While the *smṛtis* and the *purāṇas* are the bedrock of culture, Indian philosophical thought is looked upon as having two major streams, namely the *nigamas* and the *āgamas*. The *nigamas* represent the Vedic lineage of thought, and in this stream are included the six *darśanas* or schools of philosophy, which are Yoga, Vedānta, Nyāya, Vaiśeṣika, Mīmāṁsā and Sāṁkhya. It would be appropriate, though unconventional, to include Buddhist thought in this group as well. The *āgamas* are sometimes incorrectly called *Tantras*. The word *tantra* means a manual and can be applied to any manual, sacred or secular. In its religious or sacred sense *Tantra* came to mean a scripture by which knowledge is spread.[1]

While the *nigamas* accept the authority of the Vedas and can therefore be considered orthodox in their outlook, the *āgamas* represent the other stream and are quite distinctive from the *nigamas* and stand apart from the *nigamic* schools of philosophy. It is interesting that although the *āgamas* do not denigrate the Vedas, the tradition does record the displeasure of the Vaidikas about the *āgamas*. Bhattacharya notes the pejorative expressions such as the *āgamas* are "much in vogue among the low class people", the *āgamas* "were compiled to delude people fallen from the Vedic path", the followers of the *āgamas* "should be socially ostracised and that any act of social intercourse with them should be followed by expiatory rites".[2] It is right to conclude that there must have existed some tension between the followers of *āgama* and *nigama*.

The *āgamas* share a common world-view which is distinctly different from that of the *nigamas*. The ***Kulārṇava Tantra*** says that if *śruti* be the treatise for the Satya-yuga, the *smṛti* for the Tretā-yuga, the *purāṇas* for the Dvāpara-yuga the *āgamas* are for the present age or the Kali-yuga.[3] There are numerous *āgamas* and the *āgama* tradition itself is vast and complex and divided into several schools and sub-schools in all the three streams of the Śaiva, Vaiṣṇava and Śākta *āgamas*, not to speak of the Jaina *āgama* tradition. Many of the *āgamas* have been lost to the tradition over time, but they share many common ideas and concepts, so that it is possible to make some general observations about them. Etymologically, the term *āgama* suggests an ancient flow or movement (*āgamana*) as if they were a timeless river of culture, thought and tradition, and it is because of this that some scholars have claimed that the *āgamas*, rather than the *nigamas*, are the pristine or traditional documents of the Indian civilisation, predating others. While not questioning its prehistoric beginnings, we do not wish to enter into a chronological debate about the antiquity of the *āgamas* over the others. However, it is important to recognise that *āgamas* trace its lineage to pre-classical Indian thought.

Even in spite of its pre-classical origins the *āgamas* are considered orthodox rather than heterodox treatises, and as such they accept the authority of the Vedas and therefore are an integral part of the Indian tradition. However, it becomes obvious, that while accepting the authority of the Vedas and the Upaniṣads, the *āgamas* developed their own unique vision and ideas, which could best be called earthy and autochthonous rather than refined, measured or restrained, the latter terms best seem to characterise the Idealism of the forest discourses of the Upaniṣads. The ambience of the *āgamas* is spontaneous rather than contemplative, joyous rather than reasoned, outgoing rather than inward and effervescent rather than subdued, practical rather than esoteric and life-affirming rather than life-denying. The *āgamas* not only dissociated themselves from the nihilistic early Bauddhas but equally from the *nirguṇa* and passive *brahman* of the Advaita Vedāntins. Early in its evolution plastic anthropomorphic images, and not merely poetic images that the Vedas and the Upaniṣads sponsored, became important to the *āgamavādins*, and one way of characterising the *āgamas* would be to call it a culture of images rather than of words. For, the creation, the enjoyment, the celebration and the deep understanding of images is in many ways the foundational premise of the *āgamas*. This culture of images underscores the importance of sensuality in all its varied aspects, for a plastic image, if it is to be celebrated, has to be sensually cognised and enjoyed. The *āgamas* stress not only the mind as an *indriya* and as an instrument of perception, but equally the importance of the other five *indriyas* as well, and insist that all the six *indriyas* must partake in the integral enjoyment of the images. Pupul Jaykar correctly states that "the āgamas with its links to the earth, to agricultural magic and ploughing and to alchemy with its attitudes grounded in minute observation of inner and outer phenomena, as well as its concern with transformation of energy, within the mind and in the crucibles of the laboratory, gave to the artisan craftsman a vocabulary of space, colour, sound and density—the ingredients of all form."[4]

Total sensual involvement with the world and with images in particular, and in a spirit of joyousness, affirmation and celebration, is the watchword of the *āgamas*. Further the *āgamas* are equally concerned with the correct rituals with which these images are to be approached and celebrated. A common perception, therefore, about the *āgamas* are that they are manuals of image worship or temple rituals. And this is not totally incorrect, for the emphasis on images in the *āgamas* is definitely in sharp contrast to the Vedic-*vedāntic* stream of thought which is, mainly, if not entirely, non-anthropomorphic and aniconic. It is this emphasis on images that clearly makes the *āgamas* sharply different from the Vedas and Vedānta, and suggests that while the *nigamas* can be considered the expression of classical and restrained thought, the *āgamas* do contain elements that seem to originate from the non-Vedic or the pre-classical or the folk stream of the Indian tradition. This folk stream of the Indian tradition is very often dismissed as the 'little' tradition or the *deśī* tradition as compared to the 'great' or the *mārgī* or the classical tradition, and the implication very often is, that besides promoting magic and folklore, the folk tradition does not contain any sustained metaphysical ideas. This is obviously incorrect for the folk tradition gives strong hints and subtle signs of a sophisticated world-view, albeit not in a sytematic and didactic manner. The emphasis and celebration of images of the folk tradition is in sharp distinction to the non-anthropomorphic ethos of the Vedas as exemplified by the Vedic *yajña.* It is well-known that the folk stream of the Indian tradition, as seen in the Indus Valley Civilisation, emphasised the creation and celebration of images and it would be fair to assume that it is this penchant and culture for the making and enjoyment of images of the folk tradition, along with the telling of stories, that was incorporated into the *āgamas* and from the *āgamas* spilled over into the *nigamas.* Here we have a clear example of Sanskritisation within the Indian tradition, where an idea that flourishes in the folk stream is picked up, refined and transformed, and made to blend with the classical stream. This cross pollination between the two streams, the folk and the classical, continues throughout the tradition, and persists even into modern times.

The joyous, celebratory ethos of the *āgamas*, centered around images, is the undercurrent of the folk culture. The folk tradition, it has been said, is expressive and exudes energy, while the classical tradition is restrained and contemplative. Scholars have remarked on the effervescence and ebullience of the folk tradition in its various aspects. Blackburn and Ramanujan have noted that "The volatile energy in folk traditions poses a psychic counterpoint to the maintenance of control in classical traditions".[5] Not only in its content, but equally in its diffusion, is the folk culture different from the classical, and this difference can be seen between the divergent world-views of *āgamas* and the *nigamas*. But lest it be understood that the folk and the classical are two different and opposing cultures of the tradition, it should be said that the two are more a continuum rather than in opposition, more like the two banks of the same river, rather than two different rivers, in other words two parallel streams of thought.

This bubbling joyousness that one encounters in the *āgamas* is emphasised even by Patañjali in the ***Yogasūtras***, when he says the elevation of the mind to a state of bliss is indeed the quintessence of *yoga*.[6] And the ***Vijñānabhairava*** echoes a similar sentiment when it declares[7] that the mind should be fixed where it finds happiness. The ebullience and joyousness was and still remains, a quintessential feature of both folk and the *āgamic* tradition. However while emphasising the creation and celebration of images, it would be incorrect to dismiss the *āgamas* as mere manuals of image worship or temple culture, as is sometimes done, for the *āgamas* do incorporate a unique and powerful epistemology, albeit in a cryptic form. It is true that the *āgamavādins* do not set up a formal system of epistemology, but in their concern to initially assert and then transform the finite into the infinite, there are unmistakable suggestions of a singularly different world-view and epistemology. It was left to later and organised schools of philosophy within the *āgamic* tradition, like the Kāśmīr Śaivites, to develop a sophisticated and formal corpus of epistemology based on the hints that the *āgamas* contained. While the *āgamas* are not a homogeneous corpus of treatises, they however do share certain seminal epsitemic ideas and it is important to recognise them at this stage.

The world for the *āgamavādins*, as it is perceived by the senses, is real and no part of it is fictitious or illusory and therefore it is something that has to be accepted, experienced and joyously affirmed. The *āgamas,* first and foremost, were manuals of worldly and material knowledge, and only later was spiritual knowledge considered. A common teaching in the *āgamas* is for the common people to carry out their occupation with sincerity and dexterity and this then would lead to liberation. The *āgamas* appealed mainly to the simple people of the land and popular cults and rituals, rather than speculation about ultimate reality, became an important part of its teachings. Fertility and growth were of great importance to these primitive people and it therefore found a pride of place in the *āgamas* and was later reflected in the many images that they made. Thus while the Upaniṣads spoke of two birds of the selfsame feathers, one eating sweet fruit and the other watching, referring to the *nirguṇa brahman,* folk artists on the other hand show two birds sitting close together beak to beak with obvious suggestions to fertility and growth. This emphasis on growth readily explains the cult of the Mother Goddess which is an important part of the *āgamas* and which has prehistoric roots as is seen in the figures of the Indus Valley Civilisation. Bhattacharya is right in pointing out that the *nigamic* stream of thought remained aloof from the real world and withdrew from its responsibilities. They created "the illusion of pure knowledge, a form of transcendental wisdom in which world and worldly action had no place."[8]

Since the world for the pre-classical tradition was real and in no way illusory, the *āgamas* therefore set up this initial duality between the cognising subject on the one hand and the world around so that this world could be understood, affirmed and celebrated. This duality between the cognising subject and cognisable objects, between the *aham* and the *idam*, between the "I" and the "this", is the foundational premise of the *āgamas*. Since recognition, affirmation, celebration and enjoyment is the watchword of the *āgamas*, they stress that no experience or enjoyment of the world can be possible without a distinct duality between the subject and the object, and that it is this duality that leads to *savikalpa jñāna*, and that further this *savikalpa jñāna* is the result of "knowledge being enlivened by *vimarśa*"[9] Abhinavagupta defines *āgama* as the inner activity of Śiva.[10] Indian art recognises that even a sensuous *madanikā* or a *yakṣī* needs to create this duality by holding up a mirror in front of her to experience her own beauty, for without the duality created by the mirror she would not be able to enjoy her own beauty. It is important to note that the mirror in the hand of the *madanikā* creates this all important duality. The *āgamas* abhor both stark voidness and equally discourage bland oneness, and strenuously promote diversity, multiplicity and differentiation, for that is the nature of the mundane world. For voidness, according to the *āgamas*, would be unproductive of *śabda* or determinate thought and therefore, could not lead to enjoyment. In their quest for the ultimate, the *āgamas* do not ignore the immediate, but rather encourage the acceptance, understanding and enjoyment of the immediate, a process that leads to *savikalpa jñāna*. While certain *āgamic* schools, like the Śaiva Siddhānta, persist with the initial duality and go on to set up a thoroughgoing dualistic epistemology, the strongly *advaitic* Kāśmīr Śaivites start with the initial *dvaita* and transform it into a rich and joyous *advaita* through their unique and integral epistemology. Abhinavagupta states that the task of the *āgamācārya* is to explain the exact nature of the objective world and making the universe an object of knowledge.[11] This duality becomes a cornerstone in the *āgamic* epistemology.

While the transformation of the immediate to the ultimate or the movement from the apparent to the real is the basis of many schools of thought in the Indian tradition, especially the schools of the Idealist mould, the *āgamas,* while maintaining the Idealist stance, assert that this transformation is achieved through a microcosm-macrocosm homology. In other words, it is only the assertion and realisation of the immediate that can lead us to the ultimate, the finite cannot be by-passed in our quest fot the infinite, and the apparent cannot be dismissed in our drive towards the real. For, the *āgamas* declare, "what is here is elsewhere, what is not here, is nowhere".[12] The *āgamas* assert that not only is the "life of the individual an expression of the same laws which govern the universe"[13] but that *brahman* is equally *saguṇa* as well as *nirguṇa*, content-rich until the penultimate stages of realisation, even though contentless, and thus that *brahman* is to be sensually grasped. The *āgamas* stress that it requires spiritual discipline or *sādhanā* to grasp the *saguṇa brahman*, and the *āgamas* prescribe a variety of *sādhanās* for that purpose. For the *āgamavādins*, the reading or recitation or repetition of the *śāstras* is useful only if it leads to direct experience. The ***Kulārṇava Tantra*** recommends that after the essence of the scriptures are understood they should be put aside, just as he who has threshed out the grain throws away the husks and straw.[14] While in its generic sense *sādhanā* can be applied to any disciplined activity, *sādhanā* in the *āgamic* sense means joyous, creative activity. Sometimes also called *kriyā, sādhanā* or disciplined creative activity directed towards the realisation of the *saguṇa brahman* becomes the defining feature of the *āgamas*. The *āgamas* therefore promote the *sādhaka* or the seeker as a dynamic person who engages in *kriyā* or creative epistemic activity and not just passive contemplation centred on a somnolent *brahman.* Woodroffe is correct when he says that "The Śākta, above all, is a practical and active man, worshipping the Divine Activity; his watchword is *kriyā* or action."[15] Rawson sees a *sādhaka* as someone who is "rousing all the energies he can discover in his body, emotions and mind and combining them into a vehicle which will carry him towards enlightenment."[16]

Some scholars[17] point to *parivṛtti* as the key to the *āgamas* and their outlook. There are shades of meaning in the term *parivṛtti*, meanings such as 'backward look' 'turning back up' or 'turning around'. Abhinavagupta in answering a question as to how the highest reality is to be realised says that "*siddhi* is the acquisition of *ānanda* by *parivṛtti*".[18] We have Jaideva Singh's exposition of the term *parivṛtya* when he says that "it is the entire objective manifestation appearing as 'this' abiding in the full blaze of perfect 'I'-consciousness of the divine."[19] Jaideva Singh gives the etymology of the term *parivṛtya* and the concept of the fragment returning to the whole plays an important part in maintaining unity in the midst of diversity and of creating a biune unity."[20] Not only does the process of *parivṛtya* maintain the bonafides of the objective world but it leads the subject to a state of *viśrānti* or epistemic rest. The Kāśmīr Śaivite epistemology gives pride of place to this important concept of *viśrānti*, a state where the seeking, questioning mind seeks no more and comes to a state of psychic rest.

It is important to note that *parivṛtya* does not tolerate the concept of illusion neither does it have room for negation. It is the process of affirmation and then turning back, and not turning back having discovered an illusion. A popular folk-tale which has been incorporated into a favourite *pūjā*, revolves around a merchant and his son who go on a mission and return home with a shipful of gold but run into some problems when they land on the shore. *Parivṛtya* is the process of the merchant going out into the world, returning home with wealth, and then resting at home with the wealth. The extended metaphor in this story is obvious and we will expound on the underlying epistemic concept later. The process of *parivṛtya* can only come after a full and satisfactory evaluation of the object, not by a single cognition but repeated cognitions, driven not by harbouring any ideas of illusion but of reality. This concept of repeated cognitions or cognition through recognition is technically called *pratyabhijñā* and is a pivotal concept of Kāśmīr Śaivites. We will exposit how this process of *paravṛtti* stems from *pratyabhijñā* or recognition and thence forms the basis of *spandana* or vibration and thereby becomes the foundational premise of the Kāśmīr Śaivite epistemology. Interwoven in the concept of *paravṛtti* and *pratyabhijñā* is the notion of remembering what was once forgotten. *Smaraṇa* or the act of remembrance not only brings to light what was once forgotten but produces an exhilaration at finding something that was once considered lost. Here the *āgamas* draw upon the favourite and often used narrative technique of the *nāyaka* falling in love with the *nāyikā*, then forgetting the *nāyikā* and then rediscovering her after a lapse of forgetfulness when he sees some sign. We shall see later how this becomes an important epistemic tool in the hands of Kāśmīr Śaivites.

What becomes clear is that the *āgamas,* at one level are simple and close to the earth and are indistinguishable from folklore but at the same time they have unmistakably hints of a strong metaphysics and epistemology. It is as if the earthen drum of the *āgamas* can also beat a celestial rhythm.

Another feature of the *āgamas* which distinguishes them from the *nigamas* is that they are egalitarian in their outlook. The grounding principle for the *āgamas* is *samatā* or equality. It has rightly been said that *āgamic* knowledge does not belong to any person or group.[21] There was no attempt to limit the scriptures to the elite or the learned. For the *āgamas,* the reality of *bhairava* is apparent everywhere even among the common folk.[22] The ethos of the *āgamas* is comparable to a folk festival in an Indian village, where all are invited, and no one is excluded, and everyone gets involved in the celebration, whether it be a marriage or a temple festival. Unlike the Vedas which are couched in twilight language using the Sanskrit facility of *śleṣa*, the *āgamas* are open, plain, direct and simple. What they lack in erudition and refinement they more than make up in a certain joyousness and spontaneity. They exude an earthy sincerity, a desire to include each and everyone, a keenness to make the teachings of the *āgamas* available to all sections and strata of society. Nowhere do we find mention of the *varṇāśrama dharma*, neither any hint of the hierarchy of society, an idea which was an issue with Vaidikas. The *sādhaka* was told not to have an attitude of aversion nor attachment towards anyone.[23] For the *āgamas* there is no situation where Śiva is not, for wherever the mind goes, whether towards the exterior or towards the interior, everywhere there is the state of Śiva.[24] This egalitarian attitude of the *āgamas* does not merely have sociological implications but an equally strong metaphysical bearing as well. When a *sādhaka* realises that the same self-consciousness resides in all bodies, the apparent difference between subject and object starts disappearing and a foundation for a joyous, rich and affirmative *advaita* is laid.[25] For, the *āgamas* uphold, rather than reject, multiplicity, and it is in the affirmation, celebration and realisation of this multiplicity that the concept of *śakti*, so important and dear to the *āgamavādins*, is to be understood.

And finally because of the recognition and importance given to an integral and sensual perception of the world, the *āgamas*, more than the *nigamas*, become not only the vehicle of a unique metaphysics and world-view but equally the harbinger of culture in the Indian tradition. For the *āgamas,* supreme delight can arise only upon meditation of the perfect condition of joy.[26] And this joy arises from a multiplicity of sources such as the pleasure of eating and drinking, seeing a relative or a friend after a long time, the bliss of music and the delight of sexual union.[27] These and other sensual delights form the core of the folk culture which was later incorporated into the temple culture and especially in the *raṅga-maṇḍapa* or the theatre of the temple. It is here in the *raṅga-maṇḍapa* that the senses are indulged and enriched and the mind elevated to a state of excitement, it is here that musicians and dancers gather, it is here that the sculpted *madanikās* and the *kinnaras* shine in their glory, it is here that the sounds of drums and music are heard, it is here that the multiplicity of the world is understood and affirmed, it is here that *śiva-śakti-sāmarasya* takes place, it is here that the *ānanda-tāṇḍava* is performed, it is here that the *āgamas* are experienced and not merely heard, and it is here that the rich and joyous meaning of *śivatva* is understood, it is here that the *sādhaka* exclaims, "I am Śiva, with the universe as my body, and my consciousness is full and blissful."[28] And by bringing the entire objective experience to rest in the subjective self the *sādhaka* worships Śiva by becoming Śiva.[29]

Chapter 3

Mythic Images in the Indian Tradition

The Indian tradition is one of images rather than of words and therefore myth rather than history is the central plank of Indian thought, and further it would not be wrong to say that the ability to enjoy and celebrate a myth is the very essence of Indianness. It is because of this that myth as an aesthetic tool, in the Indian tradition does not need a defence, neither an analysis, and certainly not an explanation, but what it needs is a celebration. In choosing a mythopoeic rather than a historical and rational view of life the Indian tradition immediately acquires the ambience of poetry and therefore demands a poetic, rather than a rational, interpretation and enjoyment. To do otherwise would be to introduce a degree of profanity in the artistic process. Although the myths are cast in anthropomorphic terms the human facade of the myth should not disguise the cosmic dimension of the narrative, nor should it dull our sensitivity in being satisfied with a mere psychological or sociologic understanding of a particular myth. For, to do so, would be to stay on the surface and not scale the heights that the myth urges us to do. It has been rightly said that "the first function of a mythology . . . is to awaken in the individual a sense of awe, wonder and participation in the inscrutable mystery of being."[30]

Myth not only forms the bedrock in the Indian tradition of a *saguṇa* or a conceptual *brahman*, it also underpins religious practices and is at the same time the main inspiration for classical art in India. The *bhakti sampradāya* tradition in India has developed principally around the three Purāṇic mythic figures of Śiva, Viṣṇu and Śakti and secondarily around those of Sūrya and Gaṇeśa. While mythic images form the foundation of the classical tradition it is important to remember that we in India have had a strong pre-mythic and pre-literate tradition as well. These primitive people of the *deśī* or the folk tradition were prolific image makers, as is witnessed in the many images of the Indus Valley Civilisation and in rural India even today. They made images of fertile mother goddesses and of tree nymphs, *yakṣas* and *yakṣīs* and of *nāgas* and bulls. These images were not myth-based but what they lacked in their narrative content, they amply made up in their robustness and spontaneity. While classical art is driven by *artha* or meaning, folk art is driven by *śraddhā* or faith. Fertility was their dominant theme, whether it was in the images of the mother or tree goddesses or of two birds on a branch. Devoid as they are of *śāstric* injunctions, or an underlying myth, and therefore meaning, these images lacked aesthetic credentials for the classicists. These primitive images were utilitarian and played an important part in the magico-religious culture of these people. It is interesting to note that such preliterate images are still being made by the contemporary *ādivāsīs* and the tribals of India and are making a comeback in the post-modernist art of India. Out of many possible examples of these image makers are the Bustars of Madhya Pradesh in present-day India.

The central concern of classical art, as opposed to preliterate or *deśī* art, is the depiction in word or plastic image, song or dance, of myth in its manifold aspects. It is interesting to note that while the Buddha discouraged anthropomorphic depiction of himself and stressed rationality, as early as the first century BC, Aśvaghoṣa mythified Buddha's life in the ***Buddhacarita*** and later Buddhism was to become replete with myths and images.

Many Western mythologists feel comfortable to look upon myth as a metaphor or *lakṣaṇā*. Perhaps this is all they are capable of doing. They entertain *abhidhā* or the primary or the expressed meaning only briefly, and experiencing perhaps a breakdown of this primary meaning elect to settle for a metaphorical meaning. The nature of metaphor is such that the new meaning having lost all connection with the primary meaning offers only a limited secondary meaning, open only to psychological or sociological interpretations. Metaphor is a weak poetic device useful in conveying limited poetic images. The expression "Devadatta is a tiger" performs its task in drawing our attention to the tiger-like attributes of Devadatta but having done that stops short of taking us any further in our explorations. Metaphor is perhaps adequate for a *kāvya* but not for a *mahākāvya* or a mythic narrative.

The inability to move beyond metaphor is the handicap of the modern psyche relying as it does on rationality. To a mythopoeic psyche, with its own integral view of reality, there is never a breakdown of primary meaning and therefore the question of a limited metaphoric meaning never arises. To such a mythopoeic mind the reality of myth is never in question. That mythopoeic mind, and those of us who are able to handle and enjoy a myth, the aesthetic device of *dhvani* or suggestion, also sometimes called an extended metaphor, is the way to handle a myth or mythic art. While some would consider *dhvani* as just another variety of metaphor, there are significant differences in *dhvani* as opposed to *lakṣaṇā* or the limited metaphor for us to consider *dhvani* as a distinct figure of speech. While *dhvani* shares with *lakṣaṇā* the change in primary meaning, this primary meaning in *dhvani* is not totally rejected, as it is in *lakṣaṇā*, but gradually transformed into a new meaning. This new meaning is not just a single new meaning but a series of meanings, like a pile of lotus leaves held on a needle.[31]

Either religiously, through the prescribed *bhakti* practices of the *sampradāya*, or through its *rasas*, the quintessential Indian mind, celebrates and participates, rather than engages in an analysis of a myth. The celebration of myth through *bhakti* practices is outside the scope of this essay, although it forms an important part of the tradition, and for *bhaktas* the only part. Our concern is to explore avenues for the aesthetic enjoyment of the Śiva-Pārvatī myth through *dhvani* or an extended metaphor rather than a limited metaphor. To the aesthete Śiva and Pārvatī are real and so are their human and superhuman acts and experiences. There is nothing unreal about Śiva's abode in Kailāsa, his cosmic powers, his erotic and ascetic habits. And equally real for the mythopoeic mind of the aesthete is Pārvatī, her exquisite beauty, her overwhelming desire to possess Śiva, her austerity in winning Śiva's attention and her eventual marriage to him. For that mythopoeic mind, adept in the dynamics of *dhvani*, wanders at ease from the heights of Kailāsa to the depths of Pātāla, from events cosmic to matters mundane, from the realms of atemporal and the sacred, to matters profane and time-bound, and affirming every level of meaning and rejecting none, refusing to let the limitations of the rational mind impose its own judgements on it, not yielding to arid intellectual reactions, participating in every level of mythic events and the variety of meanings it offers. This fullness, catholicity and integrality is the hallmark of the mythopoeic mind, vast in its reaches and grand in its sweep, that sees no contradiction between sacred and secular, that roams in spaces above and beyond the realms of rationality, that will not let itself be truncated, for it craves wholeness, that will not permit itself to be broken into fragments, for such is the wont of a rational mind, that not only allows *lakṣaṇā* but will entertain *dhvani*, that recognises an initial duality of subject and object but enjoys the underlying *advaita* even in the midst of *dvaita*, that can hold multiple meanings as a needle holds layers of lotus leaves. Such a mythopoeic mind does not hanker after rationality or meanings at the cost of integrity, and can entertain faith and reason, transcendence and immanence, celestial and earthly, the dreamy and the wakeful at the same time. Such a mythopoeic mind is capable of dialectic thinking, capable of holding two opposite ideas in its catholic sweep. To such an artistic mind, *lakṣaṇā* or a limited metaphor, as a mode of understanding is a mere courtesan in the kingdom of myth. We are sure that when Harman refers to the qualities of a metaphor he is referring to *dhvani* for he says:

> "metaphors when they are sustained can reveal new realities. . . they are not literal statements but neither are they flowery flights of the imagination. . . they have meaning in large part because they invite us to think about one subject in the context of another. They propose a way of conceptualising which may well provide valuable insight, and at least, they permit us to think about the less familiar in terms of the more familiar. That is why it makes sense to use metaphors and to

> sustain them when we speak about more abstract matters. . . It is an important feature of metaphor that, if the metaphor is a good one, in appreciating it one goes well beyond the bare formulation of the utterance. . . This is to respond to the dynamics of a good metaphor. . . appreciation of the metaphor involves more than the simple given."[32]

It becomes clear that when Harman talks of a sustained or a good metaphor he is referring to *dhvani*, and it is in the context of *dhvani* that we are to enjoy the Śiva-Pārvatī myth, and especially their marriage, if we are to participate in the mythic event fully.

While the Vedas demonstrate some myth formation, myth as the foundation of the Indian tradition comes into its own in the epics and specially in the Purāṇas. It is fruitless to seek the basis of Purāṇic myths in history although both history and even geography must indeed colour the contents of the mythic narrative. It also goes without saying that the seeds of the Purāṇas are pre-historic. Any connection between myth and history is only of passing interest to an aesthete. Questions such as whether or not Kṛṣṇa resembles some folk hero or Śiva some Himalayan *yogī* are puerile and unnecessary. For our interest is to enjoy the myth in its grandeur, to follow every suggestion that arises from the myth and let it lead us to newer and vaster vistas, and having enjoyed the vista, return to the myth and find that the whole experience has not fragmented the myth in any sense.

If *rasa*, understood as aesthetic emotion, and *rūpa* understood as aesthetic form, are the defining features of classical Indian art, myth is its narrative basis. *Rasa* and *rūpa* alone are capable of leading a prepared aesthete to transcendent levels of *ānanda* and are rightly looked upon as *rasa-brahman* and *rūpa-brahman*. Based on this premise, pure aesthetic experience, outside the strict confines of religion, has been looked upon as a *yoga* in its own right.[33] The *rasa* doctrine as enunciated by Bharata and richly supported by *rasavādins* such as Ānandavardhana and Abhinavagupta, and countless others, was the earliest aesthetic doctrine in the Indian tradition and remains even today a powerful, foundational, secular, non-sectarian doctrine in the field of Indian art, and has a secure place in Indian aesthetics. It is the touchstone of Indian art and aesthetic experience. At the same time the numerous *śilpa-śāstras* and texts such as the ***Vastusūtropaniṣad*** and ***Viṣṇudharmottara Purāṇa*** have similarly placed the formal structural aspects of Indian art, such as its outer structure as well as its inner logic of composition, on a sound footing, capable of affording a meaning to a prepared aesthete in its own right. The *śilpa-śāstras* have ensured that a proper understanding of the superficial sensual aspects of the art object as well as its *yantra* by themselves are capable of leading the aesthete to higher realms of experience. Both *rasa* and *rūpa* remain outside the realm of religion understood as ritual. It is on the basis of this that aesthetic experience can be considered a bonafide *yoga*. In positing *brahmānanda*, albeit of the *sahodara* variety, as the end point of a sustained and penetrating aesthetic exeprience, the Indian tradition has not only recognised the value of aesthetic experience but set up a parallel avenue, parallel to the commonly understood religious practices, for transcendent realisation by an aesthete. This is important as it not only confers a certain epistemic bonafides to art but clearly suggests that religion, as narrowly defined and understood, need not be the only recourse for those who seek *rasānanda*, or aesthetic bliss through our mythic images. It asserts that the joyous realisation of art is not only an integral part of life but can be made a deeply meaningful and chastening experience, that *jñāna* need not be confined to what is sacred, or be derived from a *nirvikalpa*, abstract contemplation, but can stem from the *savikalpa* and sensuous enjoyment of an art object, and that there is a certain sanctity about the creative process within man. For creativity, both for the artist and the aesthete, is the essence of art and aesthetic experience, and in recognising art as a *yoga* we are equating *jñāna* with creativity and recognising that it is an active knowledge gaining process rather than a *vedāntic* passive removal of ignorance. The creation and realisation of art, has been, and will remain, in the Indian tradition, an exalted experience, consorting with every aspect of Indian life, but yet at the same time retaining its freedom for itself and its followers.

If *rasa* and *rūpa* give aesthetes the bonafides and the freedom to explore and experience the art object, the enjoyment and understanding the many meanings of myth, gives the aesthete yet another dimension of aesthetic enjoyment that enhances the ultimate aesthetic experience. An aesthete is primarily concerned about converting the sensation and the stimuli generated by the art object into a knowledge experience and therefore one of his interests in exploring the mythic basis of an art object is to see if it affords another vista. He is delighted if he finds, hidden with the layers of the myth, some epistemic suggestions. This discovery endears not only the myth to the aesthete, but equally the art object which speaks of this myth to that aesthete. The art object then not only remains the messenger of the myth but becomes a visual paradigm of at least some of the salient features of that epistemology. The silent gods of the art object then begin to speak to him and become a happy intermediary between the myth on the one hand and epistemology on the other. The connection between the myth and the epistemology is indeed serendipitous and this further enhances the entire experience, the myth reinforcing the epistemology, the epistemology pointing in turn to the myth, and in the process of going from one to the other the aesthetic experience is richly enhanced. This connection between a myth on the one hand and a vision of certain epistemic system on the other is not one which the tradition speaks of, and in that sense, and there is no question that in finding this interesting connection between myth and epistemology one is treading on virgin territory. In view of this the aesthete must indeed make a strong case, for he is likely to be overruled by traditionalists, or by those who take a superficial or narrow view of the myth and the art object. But for an aesthete who is steeped in the myth on the one hand and the art object on the other making this connection is hard to resist. This interconnection in no way detracts from, but rather reveals the strength of, a myth, for after all a myth is not a simple story but a narrative with cosmic dimensions and multiple meanings and it is not surprising that one discovers newer and wider meanings embedded in the myth. And finding a newer meaning does not in any way eliminate other meanings that flow from the myth, or tamper with the original myth, for one has not taken recourse to metaphor to arrive at this new meaning. The word metaphor in its Greek origin meant "to carry across" and is a figure of speech that merges two seemingly different objects or ideas. Happily for us the myth and the epistemology are not different or disparate although they appear in different garbs, the myth as a narrative and the epistemology as a discourse, and one does not need a metaphor to bring them together but a mere suggestion helps in uncovering for us a relationship that lay hidden all along.

Chapter 4

The Śiva-Pārvatī Myth

Of the many myths of Śiva that of his marriage to Pārvatī is central and one that has inspired artists and intrigued Western mythologists. A large number of strikingly beautiful amorous and anthropomorphic images of Śiva and Pārvatī pervade the tradition and are found in a variety of media and cut across various cultural and geographical boundaries within the country. No period in the history of the tradition remains unaffected by the marriage and the loving togetherness of Śiva and Pārvatī, and there is hardly any doubt that this consortship, more than any other, has deeply touched our artists.

The consortship of Viṣṇu and Lakṣmī is no doubt of importance in the tradition but there are significant differences between the two consortships, the iconography and their meanings. Champakalakshmi traces the origin of Lakṣmī to the Vedas and emphasises that Lakṣmī or Śrī has come to mean beauty, luck, wealth and prosperity. Besides, Śrī is also identified as a consort of Indra, Soma and Kubera. And more importantly Lakṣmī assumes an independent role in the pantheon with her manifestation as *aṣṭalakṣmī* which once again emphasises her material aspects such as *dhana, dhānya, dhairya, śaurya, vidyā, kīrti, vijaya* and *rājya*, underscoring the idea "that all material possessions in the world giving prosperity to the possessor are the varied aspects of Lakṣmī."[34] In her form as Gajalakṣmī she makes a strong association with water, lotus and elephants. When it comes to syncretic representation of Viṣṇu and Lakṣmī she appears as a *śrīvāstavā* on the right chest of Viṣṇu.

While Viṣṇu and Lakṣmī do appear together, the most striking image of this consortship is that of the *śeṣaśāyī* Viṣṇu with Lakṣmī at his feet. Another image of this consortship is that of Lakṣmī-Nārāyaṇa. One does encounter amorous images of Viṣṇu and Lakṣmī in the tradition but not as frequently as those of Śiva and Pārvatī. Lakṣmī assumes a position of importance on her own right in the Viṣṇu *sampradāya* and acquires an independent status in the pantheon which Pārvatī does not attain. And finally it is only very rarely that one encounters Viṣṇu and Lakṣmī in the androgyn form. It would therefore not be wrong to say that the consortship of Viṣṇu and Lakṣmī bears no resemblance to that of Śiva and Pārvatī in its myths, artistic representations and its meanings, and it is therefore safe to assert that the consortship of Śiva and Pārvatī is unique.

In its barest essence the Śiva-Pārvatī myth begins with the *devas* approaching Brahmā with the vexed problem of the demon Tāraka who is a threat to the three worlds. Brahmā decides that it is only Śiva who can vanquish Tāraka and that for this purpose he must be drawn away from his ascetic practices. The only way of doing this would be to seduce him and for this task Brahmā chooses the mountain-King Parvata. Satī, the first consort of Śiva, enters the womb of Menā, the wife of Parvata, for even as she immolated herself in the *yajña* of her father Dakṣa, she had promised that she would return to be Śiva's consort once again. Menā gives birth to Pārvatī, who even before she was born, knew that she was destined to be Śiva's consort. Pārvatī was an exquisitely beautiful and spiritually adept child and spent her childhood in the pleasant surroundings of her father's mountain kingdom. When she had reached maturity Parvata prepares her and takes her to Śiva and approaches him to consider his daughter for marriage. Śiva, deep in his meditation, is difficult to arouse, and resents Parvata's and Pārvatī's intrusion. When Kāma discharges his arrow of flowers Śiva burns him to ashes. But when Śiva eventually pays attention to Pārvatī, he dismisses her with admonishment. Pārvatī is not discouraged and approaches Śiva again and again, for she is not only a sensual beauty but a *yoginī* in her own right. She undertakes the strictest of penance, subjecting her body to austerities. The penance of Pārvatī forms an important part of poetry as well as sculpture. Poets and sculptors alike have celebrated Pārvatī as *tapasvinī*. Many a description is given of Pārvatī's *tapas*. Eating leaves and bark of the forest (*vanyāhāra*) she surrounds herself by fire on five sides (*pañcāgni-sādhanā*) or immerses herself in water (*jaloṣitā*) or stands on one foot. In sculptural representation of Pārvatī the *pañcāgni-sādhanā* is depicted by four *agni-kuṇḍas* placed in the four cardinal directions with the sun as the fifth source of fire.

Another manifestation of Pārvatī's penance is the depiction of *kuśa* or *darbha* grass held in her hands or tied to her fingers. Other attributes of Pārvatī the *tapasvinī* are the rosary (*akṣamālā*) or the alms bowl (*kamaṇḍalu*). Being a *tapasvinī,* Pārvatī is shown devoid of ornaments with a deer skin across her left shoulder and matted locks of hair.[35]

Śiva is finally aroused and enters into a dialogue with Pārvatī where she enjoins him to give up his solitary existence and consider matrimony, for only through marriage, Pārvatī argues, will Śiva cause his meditation to reach fruition. Śiva is now attracted to Pārvatī. In order to test her virtues Śiva approaches her in the guise of a wandering monk and asks her to give up her obsession of marrying the ascetic Śiva, but Pārvatī is steadfast, at which point Śiva reveals himself and accepts Pārvatī's proposal. The marriage is arranged and the wedding is solemnised by none other than Brahmā himself. Viṣṇu gives away the bride and Lakṣmī is very much a part of the wedding party. Śiva and Pārvatī celebrate each other romantically and enjoy marital bliss. Even during their romantic interludes, while Śiva exposits the virtues of the *nirguṇa brahman* of Vedānta, Pārvatī teaches him the dualistic Sāṁkhya. The only disconcerting feature of their otherwise happy marriage is that Śiva frequently goes into periods of isolation which Pārvatī, though she understands, does not quite enjoy, and her mother Menā does not approve.

This in essence is the frame narrative of the Śiva-Pārvatī myth. As in other myths there are numerous sub-stories and side plots such as the episode of the burning and resurrection of Kāma, the lust of Brahmā during the wedding ceremony, the anguish of Menā when she sees Śiva for the first time, the excitement of the town as Śiva enters with his wedding entourage and many more.

Marriage in its ideal essence is the coming together of two separate and different individuals, preceded by courtship and followed by marital bliss, and remains one of the major life experiences or *saṁskāras* of a human being. What is noteworthy is that our gods and goddesses have consorts. However among the many consortships in our manifold myths, that of Śiva and Pārvatī is the most celebrated, and even within the Śiva-Pārvatī myths, the one about their marriage is the most endearing, and one that seems to have strong epistemic suggestions. Western mythologists have enthused over this mythic marriage of Śiva and Pārvatī and have offered psychological and sociological insights into this myth, insights which are of limited interest to us. Thus while some look upon the marriage as an ideal for humans to follow, others wonder about the apparently contradictory erotic and ascetic aspects of Śiva and find it difficult to resolve these contradictions in the framework of a marriage, and yet others are taken by the kinship aspects of the marriage. Religiously the wedding of Śiva and Pārvatī is celebrated by devotees in many different ways. Every Śiva shrine on the auspicious day of *Śivarātri* is a venue for the celebratory recreation of this mythic marriage with ritual and rejoicing, an activity which again is of limited interest to us, as our concern is mainly aesthetic rather than religious. Among others, the celebration of *Śivarātri* at Khajuraho and the Mīnākṣī temple in Tamil Nadu are worth mentioning as they not only attract a large number of devotees but the religious ceremonies are both elaborate and touching. Harman stresses that the festival rituals that are enacted at the Mīnākṣī temple "create and reinforce a conceptual reality for devotees, a reality which devotionally and theologically make sense."[36] Śiva is the honoured son-in-law, not only of Mīnākṣī's father, but of every resident of Madurai. Harman correctly points out that "kinship metaphors, especially those predicated on a marriage relationship, provide a common understanding for how a community of people may become allied to particular deity over generations. The marriage becomes the source of Śiva's relationship to Madurai devotees and it provides new ways to understand divine action."[37]

However an aesthetician, who is primarily an epistemologist, is concerned mainly with enjoying the Śiva-Pārvatī myth artistically and not religiously. The *rasika* celebrates Śiva through the narrative as in the ***Śiva Purāṇa*** and equally through the various Śiva-Pārvatī images in the tradition. His mission is to soak in the surface sensation of that myth and convert it into knowledge, rather than participate in it ritually, for he is not involved in a superficial art encounter nor a religious experience, but in a deeply meaningful and blissful art experience. Towards this end he is interested, not in explaining or analysing the art object, for to do this would prevent the art experience from reaching its full and rich fruition, neither is he interested in participating in a religious ritual. While not negating other avenues towards this mythic event he is receptive to the many levels of meaning that flow from the art object, and is able to hold these multiple meanings in an unbroken chain, but at the same time he is averse to looking upon it as a limited metaphor and offer a metaphorical analysis of the myth or the images. An aesthetician looks wonderstruck at the art object, be it a *kāvya*, *śilpa* or *citra* of Śiva and Pārvatī, which keeps on offering an endless vista of experiences, a veritable *kāmadhenu* of meanings. At the same time the Śiva-*rasika* hesitates to point out or offer explanations or analysis, lest this should disturb the rapturous state of his mind. For, it is a beautiful state of *dhyāna* or contemplation in which the aesthete's mind is settled and one that does not crave attention, where petty rational concerns and problems do not arise, where awareness moves centripetally towards the still centre of movement. A true aesthetic experience is one of a rich and radiant silence, *samāveśa*, full and integral, where the *rasika* and the *rasa* are *advaitic* where no fragmentations occur.

However while an aesthete rejects a metaphorical analysis of the art object as unaesthetic activity, he does sincerely and strenuously undertake an aesthetic analysis. For, an aesthetic analysis starts with the principle that under no account should the integrity of the art object be violated, its reality be never questioned and any meaning that stems from the analysis be held in an unbroken chain. *Advaita* is the watchword for an aesthete, and although he creates an initial duality, he ensures that in the final moments of the aesthetic experience there is no trace of that initial duality. Any analysis, of a part or the whole art object, is examined and enjoyed but referred back to the surface or the source, so that every level and shade of meaning leads to a greater enjoyment and understanding of the art object and thereby increase his aesthetic delight. It is in this spirit that an analysis of the myth and the art object are undertaken.

The concept of *parokṣārtha* or hidden and subtle meanings is part of the Indian poetic tradition and is particularly applicable to myth and mythic images. For the Vedic Indian, *vāk* was the vehicle of artistic expression, and as the *ṛṣis* themselves admitted, only a quarter of it was understandable, the rest of the three-fourths mystically lay hidden, and therefore capable of leading the adept aesthete into deeper and invisible visions of meaning by its mere suggestion. *Vāk* is exalted language, beautiful as it stands in its *sākṣāt artha* but richer in its offering of *parokṣārtha*.

It is with this background of *parokṣārtha* that an understanding and analysis of the Śiva-Pārvatī marriage myth is undertaken. Śiva and Pārvatī are not just mythic beings to be worshipped, not just symbols to be decoded, not also metaphors to be explained, but objects of beauty, richly endowed with meanings to be enjoyed. The coming together in a divine consortship is an event to be celebrated in itself by the devotee and enjoyed for its manifold meanings by the aesthete.

It is important to explore the epistemology of aesthetic experience in the Indian tradition for an aesthetician is essentially an epistemologist and his fundamental concern is to study how sensual data, generated by the art object, is led into a knowledge episode, creating a rich and true aesthetic experience. Aesthetic experience, while being one of many human experiences, is no ordinary experience for the aesthetician. It is the experience *par excellence*, the ultimate, transcendent experience, an experience of *brahma-jñāna*, and upon which rests his entire world-view. It is aesthetic experience that bridges the Śiva-Pārvatī myth on the one hand and Kāśmīr Śaivism on the other, the myth being the paradigm and the philosophical system providing the didactic exposition of that experience. The aesthetician sees the bridge as an opportunity to go from one to the other, from the myth to the philosophical system, and from the philosophical system back to the myth, thereby not only enjoying both, but letting one shed light on the other. This essentially is the premise of this essay, namely that the Śiva-Pārvatī myth on the one hand and Kāśmīr Śaivism epistemology on the other, both in their unique way provide an elucidation of aesthetic experience. The aesthetician is deeply committed to this task and is not content to merely partake of the joyous experience of the bridge but needs to explore the entire gamut of the tradition to ensure that there are no other such bridges. Without that exploration within the tradition it would not be possible to make a claim for that bridge. One must explore every system of philosophy that can provide a philosophic undergirding for aesthetic experience, to find a philosophic system that gives credence not only to the experiencing subject but equally to the art object, a system that values creativity on the part of the artist and the aesthete alike, that maintains an *advaitic* link between the subject and the object, and which ensures that no sectarian dogma nor theology touches the epistemic process. For the aesthete it is of fundamental importance that an aesthetic experience be underpinned by a philosophic system and that too of the Idealist mould, for Idealism ensures a complete and contemplative enjoyment of the art object. Sri Aurobindo is right when he says:

> "the whole basis of Indian artistic creation perfectly conscious and recognised in the canons, is directly spiritual and intuitive. . . its highest business is to disclose something of the Self, the Infinite, the divine. . . (The Indian artist does not depend on) an idea in the intellect, a mental imagination, an outward emotion. . . (but instead dips into an) . . . idea, image, emotion of the spirit. . . This is the distinctive character of Indian art and to ignore it is to fall into total incomprehension or into much misunderstanding. . . And it is because of this that the ordinary aesthetic instinct will not suffice, a spiritual insight or culture is needed if we are to enter into the whole meaning of Indian artistic creation."[38]

The word *artha* or meaning sums up the entire undercurrent of *mārgī* artistic activity, just as *śraddhā* is the defining feature of a religious experience. Aesthetic meaning is to be grasped not by the senses or intellect alone but by direct intuition as well; and unless the art object, through its *rasa* and *rūpa*, is propelled to its ultimate meaning through the dynamics of *dhvani*, the artistic encounter remains a sterile, incomplete, superficial and hedonistic experience. It is the function of the aesthete to seek and realise artistic meaning up to the fullest through *rasa* and *rūpa* on the one hand and through the suggestions of the underlying myth on the other.

Art, as revealed both through the myth and the images, precedes aesthetics, and the proper understanding and realisation of what is created cannot be done in isolation from the creative process itself. The major schools of Indian thought set their examination of the nature, value and significance of creative processes also within the framework of the quest for ultimate reality. From our perspective, it is important to note that a metaphysical system which considers creative processes to be either ultimately unreal or of little value cannot provide a firm basis for artistic experience, for an aesthete is as much of a creator as an artist.

Abhinavagupta maintains that schools of Realism, which include Sāṁkhya, Nyāya-Vaiśeṣika, Mīmāṁsā and Cārvāka, cannot provide a satisfactory basis for aesthetic experience. It is true that these schools of thought accept consciousness as an ultimate metaphysical category, but they do not perceive creativity to be an ultimate value within that consciousness. Abhinavagupta takes the position that for those who are content with the superficial and the momentary, these Realistic systems of thought will do. He implies that for those who seek to give an ultimate meaning to the objective world, and in particular to art objects, these schools of thought will not suffice.[39]

From the Idealist schools of thought, we only need to consider seriously the epistemology of Śaṅkara's Ádvaita Vedānta, for this was the first formal post-Upaniṣadic system of thought, and it was an exalted system of Indian thought even in Abhinavagupta's time. The Viśiṣṭādvaita of Rāmānuja is an important school of thought, as far as Hindu aesthetics is concerned, for it gave a prominent place to *kāvya, saṅgīta, nṛtya* and all forms of visual art within the auspices of the temple. Chronologically, Rāmānuja came much later than Abhinavagupta, and therefore we do not have Abhinavagupta's evaluation of Viśiṣṭādvaita and of the practices of *bhakti* associated with this school of thought. From our perspective, Rāmānuja's system offers only qualified support for a *yoga* of art as we intend to pursue it. The major obstacle in Rāmānuja's Viśiṣṭādvaita, from our point of view, is the fact that for Rāmānuja, *bhakti* is the overriding principle and all epistemic experience must be subordinated to it. A pure aesthetic experience, devoid of *bhakti*, would be unacceptable to Rāmānuja and his school of thought. However, it must be admitted that Viśiṣṭādvaita, considered purely as a metaphysical system, can offer a firm ontological basis for establishing the ultimate value of aesthetic experience. Viśiṣṭādvaita affirms the reality of the world and the validity of objective experience by regarding this world as 'the body of God'. It establishes the value of all creative processes by granting them an ontological basis in the creative energy of God. And above all it grants ultimate value to beauty by perceiving it to be an essential attribute of God. But, by the same token, in practice, the *viśiṣṭādvaitins* insist that the perception of beauty should be subordinated to *bhakti*, thereby denying the art object an objectivity of its own. Strictly speaking the object in the epistemology of Viśiṣṭādvaita becomes part of the subject, and independents credentials of the object are lost, and therefore no real subject-object transaction can take place. Further, Viśiṣṭādvaita would not allow us to consider secular art objects as part of our *yoga* thereby restricting our freedom and choice. Therefore despite Viśiṣṭādvaita's involvement with art, an aesthete cannot be totally comfortable in its epistemic system, committed as he is to freedom in his choice of aesthetic experience.

Śaṅkara recognises the objective world of name and form as provisionally real, and further recognises that the perception of this objective world is a function of all beings. For Śaṅkara, this world of manifold perceiving subjects, and objects of perception, has no existence apart from *brahman*. In his metaphysics Śaṅkara recognises the world as provisionally real and in his epistemology he strongly argues that the world of objects is not a creation of the subjective mind as the Bauddhas would have it, thereby distinguishing his world-view from the *vijñānavādins*. Nevertheless in the end, he would have us insist that the universe is ultimately unreal, an appearance maintained by *avidyā* and superimposed on *brahman*, a process he calls *māyā*. Śaṅkara however does afford an objective reality to *avidyā* for he declares "*avidyākṛtam kāryaprapañcam*".[40] According to Śaṅkara, *avidyā* is not a non-entity like the son of a barren woman, but a logical, rational, way of thinking characteristic of the finite human mind. However Śaṅkara makes it amply clear that *avidyā* cannot lead us to a realisation of ultimate reality for not only is it *trikālabādhyam,* i.e., it cannot transcend the limitations of three-fold time, but it is a mere *adhyāsa*, a superimposition of the world on *brahman*. One of the major problems with Śaṅkara's epistemology is the puzzling question of the origin of *avidyā*, for we can rightly ask, "from whence does this *avidyā* arise?" As Abhinavagupta asks, "To whom does this *avidyā* belong? *Avidyā* cannot reside in *brahman,* nor in the individual, it is neither real nor phenomenal, nor both."[41] But yet Śaṅkara himself admits that a mirage cannot exist without a basis, the snake cannot exist without the rope.[42] *Avidyā*, in Śaṅkara's system, remains *anirvacanīya*, an epistemic mystery, a grand illusion, and one cannot but accept Pārthasārathi Miśra's cutting remark that "in this system (of Śaṅkara) which maintains that everything transcends explanation, unreasonableness is also no objection."[43] The other major problem with Śaṅkara's system is that the objective world of *māyā* and the ultimate *brahman* remain unrelated and fragmented without any epistemic relationship, save that of negation. In his epistemology, there is a sharp break between the perception of objects and the knowledge of *brahman*. *Brahman* for Śaṅkara, remains altogether non-conceptual.[44] The knowledge of *brahman* is a *parokṣajñāna*, intuitive non-cognitive knowledge. Śaṅkara's *brahman* is abstract, *nirvikalpa* and *nirguṇa*, at whose gates we are asked to drop every form of cognition, for Śaṅkara's *brahman* is a lion's den where all that enters is lost.[45] For, in Śaṅkara's scheme of things, after *brahman* is known, the phenomenal world becomes unreal, because for Śaṅkara, one's self is not illumined by inert objects of the world. For the realisation of that *advaya brahman* Śaṅkara prescribes pretty strong medicines,[46] for different from the world is *brahman* and other than *brahman* there is nothing. To use his own analogy there is no way, whereby the truth of the rope and illusion of the snake can be upheld at one and the same time. In the light of ultimate truth the reality of the universe is contradicted, and consequently, objects of perception, are divested of ultimate value. According to Śaṅkara, the mind that rests in the contemplation of *brahman* as well as the universe of objects at the same time is adrift like two logs in the ocean never to meet again.

From Abhinavagupta's perspective there are major problems in accepting Śaṅkara's metaphysics as a framework for aesthetic experience. Śaṅkara's *māyāvāda* ultimately rejects the world of objects and, therefore, cannot give ultimate value to the art object. Further, since Śaṅkara's *brahman* does not include the world of objects and is essentially passive and *nirguṇa*, as a consequence, all creative processes, whether in material nature or in human consciousness, including the creation and enjoyment of art, are relegated ultimately to the status of *māyā*. Therefore although Śaṅkara, unlike the Bauddhas, is not a nihilist, his epistemology in the ultimate analysis is fundamentally one of *neti-neti* or negation, rather than positive and affirmative.

Having knocked at the doors of every school of philosophy, or *darśana*, in the Indian system, the aesthete finds himself at the doors of Kāśmīr Śaivism. A sound epistemology of aesthetic experience must be grounded in a metaphysics that provides first, a firm support for objective experience as exemplified by aesthetic experience, and second, an ontological basis for affirming creativity and creation as values that are not denied or negated at any point. We need to place art experience within the orbits of a system of thought that gives credence both to the creator as well as to the connoisseur, the artist as well as the aesthete, art creation as well as aesthetic experience. In the major *darśanas*, or schools of Indian philosophy, the question of the relationship between the subject and the world of objective experience is set within the framework of the quest for ultimate reality. Radhakrishnan sums up the problem when he says, "When we divide the subject from the object, the question of building the bridge from one to the other becomes difficult. Either we have to hold that the object is the creation of the subject or that there is no object at all."[47] For, the aesthete is committed not only to the subject or *pramātā* or the knower, for indeed the knower is the driving force in any epistemic process, but equally to the *prameya* or what is to be known or the object of cognition. He cannot sacrifice one for the other, and the art object for the Kāśmīr Śaivite should not only be instrumental but inherent in the ultimate aesthetic experience. He is interested in taking on the art object as a bride, epistemically to be loved and treasured for ever, and not as a courtesan to be used and discarded after the purpose is served. Neither is he interested in using it as a boat merely to cross a river. The aesthete in choosing a home for aesthetic activity further wants to ensure that creation and creativity are considered bonafide activities and given a metaphysical basis. Kāśmīr Śaivism is the only system of philosophy that satisfies these epistemic requirements of the aesthete and he lovingly embraces it; it is there that he finds that he can rest and wander no more in search for a home. Having found a home in the epistemology of Kāśmīr Śaivism the aesthete is further thrilled when he serendipitously finds that a Purāṇic myth offers a perfect artistic illustration of that epistemology, not through *sūtras* and *mantras*, or dogma and credo, but through a beautiful narrative of a marriage. Here is the bridge that he was looking for. In discovering that the marriage of Śiva and Pārvatī, as narrated in the Purāṇas, is a perfect illustration, an artistic paradigm, of aesthetic experience, and that aesthetic experience is firmly underpinned by Kāśmīr Śaivite epistemology, the aesthete experiences not just superficial excitement but a vindication of his innermost beliefs. It is one thing to find that the tenets of Kāśmīr Śaivism uphold and undergird aesthetic experience in general, but an unbounded joy to find that a Purāṇic narrative is, as it were, a perfect illustration of those very tenets. The aesthete does realise that one is not causally connected to the other, that the Śiva-Pāravtī myth is not causally related to Kāśmīr Śaivism, but in stumbling upon a similarity, a bridge, the aesthete is indeed overjoyed. It is as if in a throng of people one accidentally runs into another person who is a perfect copy of oneself and in following this person in the crowd one learns more about oneself. An aesthete, steeped in the tenets of Kāśmīr Śaivism, enjoys those very epistemic tenets visually when participating and aesthetically celebrating the Śiva-Pārvatī myth and especially their marriage. This essay is an expression of that thrill and delight, of the joy and amazement, of an aesthete, on discovering the perfect correspondence between the epistemology of Kāśmīr Śaivism on the one hand and the marriage of Śiva and Pārvatī on the other, as revealed to us in the Purāṇas and in our arts, and each upholding the dynamics of aesthetic experience. The pleasure is further enhanced on finding that in enjoying the myth, and the art that stems from it, one is led to a better understanding of Kāśmīr Śaivism, and on reflecting upon Kāśmīr Śaivism one is led to a greater enjoyment of the myth and the art. One experience enhances the other, and in turn richly illuminates the dynamics of aesthetic experience. And fusing the two, Kāśmīr Śaivism on the one hand and the mythic marriage of Śiva and Pārvatī on the other, is the strikingly beautiful androgyn image of *ardhanārīśvara*, which captures the essence of both.

The aesthete senses the same serendipitous feeling because the image of *ardhanārīśvara* has a status of its own unrelated to Kāśmīr Śaivism. The *ardhanārīśvara* is a major image in the Indian pantheon and its origin can be traced back along with other Purāṇic images. Banerjea writes that "the iconic motif of *ardhanārīśvara* was evolved at a fairly early period . . . and glyptic and sculptural evidence (of this image is found) as early as the Kushan and Gupta periods."[48] However even though it is a major *rūpa,* scholars differ in their interpretations of this important image. Sivaramamurti writes that the "*ardhanārīśvara* suggests a unique conception of the closely knit ideal of man and woman rising above the craving of the flesh and serving as a symbol of hospitality and parenthood."[49] Banerjea feels that the *ardhanārīśvara* image "does not illustrate any particular mythology"[50] and he reads syncretism as the underlying principle of the image, and further equates it with other syncretic images such as that of Harihara and feels that the image of the *ardhanārīśvara* was created to lessen the tension between the sometimes opposing Śiva and the Śakti cults.[51] Kramrisch comments that the *ardhanārīśvara* is a "biunity of the male and female in God."[52] Pal comments that "such androgynous forms were conceived by the theologians to emphasize the bisexuality, and therefore the non-duality of the supreme being."[53] O'Flaherty states that "androgyny in its inescapably naked form . . . presents a profound human truth and not grotesque miscarriage of nature".[54]

To an aesthete, these and other such explanations are of only passing interest. Not denying the validity of these comments, he reads something distinctly different and more exciting in the singularly beautiful image of the *ardhanārīśvara*, which while depicting the togetherness of Śiva and Pārvatī in a unique and charming and visually attractive way, gives strong hints and suggestions of the epistemology of Kāśmīr Śaivism. An aesthete is taken up more by Pārvatī *vimarśinī* rather than by Pārvatī *ardhāṅginī*, the epistemic functions of Pārvatī rather than her social and ethical attributes. The *śilpa* texts vary on the number of hands that the *ardhanārīśvara* may have and also on the objects they carry. While Banerjea refers to the *darpaṇa* as one of the objects, it is Kramrisch who correctly identifies the *darpaṇa* in the Elephanta image of Śiva as *ardhanārīśvara.* Very often the *darpaṇa* like the *Nandī*, is assumed rather than actually depicted in the artistic composition. To an aesthete steeped in the epistemology of Kāśmīr Śaivism the *darpaṇa* in one of the left hands of the *ardhanārīśvara* is of great interest as it illustrates the all important concept of *pratyabhijñā* or cognition through recognition. The *darpaṇa* is singularly important to Kāśmīr Śaivites and becomes an important symbol, which in the words of Eliade "express(es) simultaneously a number of meanings whose continuity is not evident on the plane of immediate experience . . . the religious symbol translates a human situation into cosmological terms."[55] It is interesting that when human understanding and realisation is being discoursed people stumble upon Kāśmīr Śaivism without their knowledge. Pupul Jaykar, writing on insight, touches serendipitously the heart of *pratyabhijñā,* when she states:

> The movement of insight (is) a voyage into time, into the past limitless. The awakening of insight demands a seeing, listening, which is the awakening of all the senses simultaneously, so that, in that instant, fragmentation ends. The senses flowing simultaneously is a state of flowering, an awakeness, in which the barriers of the within and without cease. A state that perceives the object, the "what is", with all the senses alive, apprehends object without that perception being held or transformed by object. And so the seeing, listening, continues without obstacle to inhibit it or give it direction. This stream of per-

> ception having no banks and no intention is an instant of eternity. Insight does not search. It sees the within and the without of objects, grasps it as a whole. This seeing is the creative ground that makes luminous and reveals. In this state the holistic is the perception. Out of this arises insight and skill in action. (With) this insight and skill the manifestation and presencing of the formless is inevitable.[56]

Insight is thus a movement and understood this way *pratyabhijñā* is nothing other than holistic perception and insight. One readily echoes Kṣemarāja's sentiments when he says that "there are some devoted people who are undeveloped in reflection and have not taken pains in studying difficult works of logic" and it is for such people that the teachings have to be revealed in a short and simple form as he himself reveals the teachings of the ***Īśvarapratyabhijñā*** succinctly in the ***Pratyabhijñāhṛdayam***.[57] For an aesthete those same teachings are revealed beautifully and unequivocally through the Purāṇic accounts of Śiva and Pārvati's marriage, the image of the *ardhanārīśvara* and particularly through the *darpaṇa* in the hand of Pārvatī.

Chapter 5

The Darpaṇa of Pārvatī

It is an accepted practice to divide philosophical systems as Idealist or Realist, and even though the terms are of Western origin, they are useful even in the Indian tradition. When it comes to defining Idealism the Western tradition has been in a quagmire even at the most fundamental level. One of the main reasons for this is the basis on which the definition of Idealism is attempted. Western scholars define Idealism on an ontological basis which brings in questions of the Absolute and raises questions of value. In the Indian tradition a classification and evaluation of a system is done mainly on an epsitemic basis. Dasgupta defines Idealism as that system which recognises that the knowledge of ultimate reality is spiritual rather than material or in other words non-cognitive rather than just cognitive.[58] Realistic systems on the other hand affirm that ultimate reality is cognitive. Abhinavagupta condemns these Realistic systems and finds them useful only to "children, women and idiots".[59] Keeping in mind this admonition we must, in our endeavour to understand the mirror of Pārvatī, therefore concern ourselves only with the Idealistic systems. In order to show that the Śiva-Pārvatī myth is a perfect visual paradigm of the epistemology of Kāśmīr Śaivism it is important to explore the other two philosophical systems that share the Idealist plank, namely, Śaṅkara's Advaita Vedānta and Rāmānuja's Viśiṣṭādvaita. There are two main issues that confront the *advaitin*: the epistemic status of the object and the nature of the cognising subject, both at the microcosmic and the macrocosmic level. While Śaṅkara gives only a provisional status to the object, the Bauddhas reject the existence of the object and Rāmānuja makes the object dependent on the subject; it is only the Kāśmīr Śaivite that ensures that the object has a bonafide epistemic status of its own. Similarly the ultimate subject or *brahman* for Śaṅkara is passive and incapable of self-awareness, merely *prakāśa,* only *jñāna*, but passive and devoid of *kartṛtva* or *kriyā* or epistemic activity, which gives rise to the term *śānta-brahmavāda* to this doctrine. For Śaṅkara, *kartṛtva* or *kriyā* is a defining feature of the empirical world, born out of primal ignorance, *anirvacanīya* or undefinable, a source of ignorance and therefore cannot be a part of *brahman*. While for the Kāśmīr Śaivites, Śiva or the ultimate subject is not merely *prakāśa* but *prakāśavimarśamaya*, not just passive *jñāna* but *jñāna* along with *śakti*, not merely possessed of the knowledge "I" but equally "I am this", not merely "*aham*" but "*aham-idam*". Maheśvarānanda asserts in no uncertain terms that the *brahman* of Vedānta devoid of *sphuraṇa* or epistemic stir is as good as unreal.[60] The *sphuraṇa* of Śiva, which includes Śakti, is the essence of Kāśmīr Śaivite epistemology, the quintessence of the mythic Śiva-Pārvatī marriage, and the main *rasa* of the togetherness of Śiva and Pārvatī in various art forms. For were it not for this *spandana* Śiva and Śakti would remain like two logs adrift in the ocean.

The Kāśmīr Śaivite tradition recognises that the human condition is characterised by *āsīdekam* or primal epistemic isolation or voidness, and that if this is left unresolved it leads to a lack of self-awareness. This primal human epistemic need of self-awareness leads to a craving or desire for an initial experience of duality, underscoring the essential component of *icchā* or desire in any epistemic activity. Utpaladeva refers to this in the ***Śivastotrāvalī*** by reminding us that the old adage "one should worship Śiva by becoming Śiva" is not acceptable to him for he says that "one should worship Śiva by becoming a devotee" for as he says the true devotee recognises the non-dual aspect of Śiva while maintaining duality.[61] Utpaladeva is upholding the position of a *bhakta* rather than of a *rasika*. Creating and sustaining this duality is an essential pre-requisite both for the devotee and the aesthete. A devotee maintains this duality till the end, the aesthete however moves to non-duality after the initial duality. The aesthete, who is also driven by desire, on the other hand, starts from a *dvaitic* stage in his enjoyment of the object, but moves on to an *advaitic* stage which includes the object of his aesthetic attention.

Icchā or the epistemic desire is pivotal in Kāśmīr Śaivite epistemology. Abhinavagupta has emphasised the importance of *icchā* in no uncertain terms:

> "(The universal will) in the form of desire (*kāmanā*) blossoms forth through the individual subject. Thus actualized it is apparent as a desire for sense-objects. It does not proceed through the succeeding phases (mechanically) step by step like the feet of the blind. Rather, after it has been aroused and has initially decided upon its goal, thus stimulated, it bounds forward with delight to forcibly lay hold of its goal like a far-sighted man when walking. The will is clearly evident in the initial stage when it has (just) arisen and is similarly full and perfect (*pūrṇa*) in its final state of rest."[62]

Kāśmīr Śaivism emphasises that the desire for self-awareness cannot be solipsistic and can only be fulfilled only when there is the fervent *icchā* or desire for objective cognition. It is for this reason that Kāma was deputed to discharge his arrow, for without the desire Śiva would have remained in his solipsistic and unfruitful contemplation. For in the desireless and passive state, Śiva's consciousness is involuted as in a peacock's egg, unable to expand. It is only desire that transforms *nimeṣa* into *unmeṣa* and "differentiated awareness pours out of the body of undifferentiated consciousness, heralded by a subtle stress or vibration (*ghūrṇana*) of aesthetic delight set up in its causal matrix."[63] Desire, then is the key to the unfolding of the epistemic process. For self-awareness, according to Kāśmīr Śaivites, can come only through a perception and joyous affirmation of duality, and that eventual subjectivity requires objective affirmation, that Śiva devoid of Śakti is lifeless or a mere *śava*. It is this primal and basic need of self-awareness, through a perception of duality, that created a desire and led Prajāpati to gaze outward, *īkṣita* or *unmukhatā*, with a declaration "*bahu syāṁ prajāyeya*", may I be many, May I procreate.[64] While this statement can be understood at many different levels, our interest is primarily epistemic, and emphasises that desire is the seed of the epistemic process. An initial epistemic duality is thus recognised, early in the tradition, as the basis of life itself, for is it not Indra, who as the Prajāpati of the universe, sets up the first duality between heaven and the earth with his *indrakīla*, a duality that leads to all other dualities in the human condition? And it was Indra who ensured the success of the *ādināṭya*, the first drama, by installing the *jarjara* in the *maṇḍapa*. In traditional dramatic performances it is still an accepted practice for the *sūtradhāra* to start the dramatic proceedings with the installation of the *indrakīla*. In the world presided over by Indra, creation can survive only as long as this duality is maintained, and by extension it can be said, that knowledge can arise only when desire spurs an initial duality. In fact the desire towards, and recognition of duality is one of the primal instincts of life, it underpins creation and then becomes the basis of knowledge. Faced with this voidness, *īkṣitā* or *unmukhatā*, or the act of looking up, becomes a manifestation of the primal epistemic act that leads to all other acts, the initial epistemic step that leads towards the unfoldment of self-knowledge. The Upaniṣads while fervently maintaining their monistic outlook and recognising primal human epistemic voidness seek a reconciliation of the one and many, subject and object, knowledge and ignorance, but do not undertake to address the concept of *īkṣitā* in any sustained fashion, as they are driven towards the *nirguṇa nirvikalpa brahman*. A *nirguṇa brahman* cannot have any creative function, for creation understood even in an epistemic sense implies activity, which the *nirguṇa brahman* is incapable of. On the other hand, *unmukhatā*, or outward gazing, becomes the seed of discourse and the basis of knowledge in Kāśmīr Śaivism, as for them *brahman* is equally *saguṇa* and *nirguṇa*, and such a *brahman* has *kriyā* or creative activity and *svātantrya* or the freedom to exercise that activity, as its defining feature. *Kriyā* or epistemic desire is the direct result of *icchā*. Abhinavagupta reminds us that knowledge and activity are the very life of living beings[65] and therefore by deduction, knowledge without activity is not possible, and equally for one seeking knowledge, activity without knowledge is unthinkable. Knowledge leads to activity and activity in turn must lead to knowledge. It is important to stress that both knowledge and activity are to be understood here in its epistemic and not psychological or empirical sense. As Dyczkowski rightly points out "Monistic Śaivism . . . considers consciousness to be the basic model through which we understand Being."[66] The parallels between Kāśmīr Śaivite epistemology and the marriage of Śiva and Pārvatī are evident as it is clear that the marriage is the epistemic drama of that consciousness, and therefore a paradigm of that epistemology. Self-knowledge for the Kāśmīr Śaivites, is an active rather than a passive process; it is an *unmeṣa*, an unfolding, the nature of which is a vibration, a *spandana* of *cit*.[67] And knowledge cannot remain passive, of the *vedāntic* variety, and be devoid of activity.[68] It is said that Śiva empowered by the sweetness in the three corners of his heart, raises his face to gaze at and unfold the splendour of the universe.[69] The scripture further reminds us that this gazing outward, *unmukhatā*, creates the initial duality between subject and object and becomes the defining activity of all embodied ones, but it is only a *yogī* who while experiencing this epistemic duality is mindful of this dualistic but tentative relation.[70] For while recognising duality as the first epistemic step, the resolution of this duality into oneness is the goal of all Idealistic Indian systems, and Kāśmīr Śaivism in that Idealist mould vigorously pursues this drive towards *advaita*, in the face of an initial and provisional *dvaita*, in its own unique fashion. We join Abhinavagupta in saluting "that Śiva who having initially manifested the diversity of the universe leads it towards the ultimate reality of unity."[71] That the realisation of ultimate reality is a two-step process, brought about by an epistemic pulsation, a *spandana* of *cit*, the first tentative dualistic cognition followed by a second more refined cognition, is a fundamental tenet of Kāśmīr Śaivism epistemology, brought out beautifully by the Śiva-Pārvatī marriage and equally by the strikingly beautiful concept of *ardhanārīśvara*. This *spandana* is the divine cosmic pulsation, the eternal throb that translates *jñāna* into *kriyā* and takes *kriyā* back to *jñāna* again, enabling self-awareness; it is this *spandana* that bridges the cognising subject with the cognitive object ensuring that the two are never adrift, that propels a *rasika* to a *kāvya* and is mindful that the two should never again be separated, that unites Śiva with Pārvatī in a blissful marriage. This pulsating consciousness, the *vimarśa-spandana*, is the foundation upon which Kāśmīr Śaivism metaphysics is constructed and rests. Consciousness, joyously pulsating, is not just self-knowledge, but an all-pervasive principle that is the basis of all that is manifested. Abhinavagupta reminds us of the traditional homage paid to the "deity which at first creates the illusion for those who are deluded in the world and then dispels it, and which at first conceals the unitary bliss of pure self-consciousness and then reveals it."[72] There is thus a movement, a *spandana*, a pulsation, a throb, between an initial dualistic and later non-dualistic cognition, a *spandana* that becomes the defining feature of Kāśmīr Śaivism. As Dyczkowski correctly states "Spanda in its most fundamental form . . . is the Śaiva solution to the problem of relating the finite to the absolute"[73] and by the same token, of relating Pārvatī to Śiva. Without the *spandana* there would be no knowledge, neither self-awareness nor the romantic interlude between Śiva and Pārvatī. It is the doctrine of *spanda* that can reconcile movement and stillness, *unmīlana* and *nimīlana*, the one and the many, creation and reabsorption, subject and object. For *spanda* is nothing but the alternation of *unmeṣa* and *nimeṣa*, the opening and closing of Śiva's eyes, it is the cosmic rhythm through which the universe unfolds. *Nimeṣa* leads to *unmeṣa*, and *unmeṣa* turns around towards *nimeṣa* once again, one causing the other. This is the cosmic *spandana*, the *parivṛtti*[74] or turning around, of the fragment returning to the whole, of the *idam* returning to the *aham* and becoming *aham-idam*. *Unmeṣa* is expansion, for this is the very nature of Śiva, although deep in his contemplation he forgets this, as he spurns Pārvatī's advances. And what better way to visually depict this epistemic principle of expansion and involution, the *spandana*, than through the marriage of Śiva and Pārvatī, for in entreating Śiva to accept her in marriage, Pārvatī is only ensuring that Śiva expand his contemplation to include the fragment and then return it to the whole. Pārvatī knows only too well that "there can be only one possessor of her".[75] This cosmic marriage not only inspires artists to produce beautiful poetic and plastic images but equally through their romantic interplay has enough drama to be a paradigm of the epistemic transactions of Kāśmīr Śaivism. There is thus a dialogue, an interplay of question and answer, between Śiva and Pārvatī, the eternal subject and the consummate object, where romance and epistemology intermingle, both in the myth and in the *āgamas*. It is but fitting that we link epistemology with romance, for the joy and excitement of a cognising subject in the process of acquiring knowledge, is best reflected by the amorous relationship of Śiva and Pārvatī. There is here the presence of *śṛṅgāra rasa* but even more of an *adbhuta rasa*. The initial apprehension and hesitation, the tentative duality, the epistemic dialogue between the subject and the object, and the ultimate union of the two in a joyous epistemic experience, finds a parallel in the mythic marriage of Śiva and Pārvatī. But lest we think that Śiva and Pārvatī are two ordinary mortals or that this is a mere arid intellectual discourse, Abhinavagupta reminds us that it is Bhairava's delight in being at once the questioner and the responder.[76] We will return to this idea when we discuss the *viśrānti* of Śiva.

The Kāśmīr Śaivites use terms connected with light in their exposition. Thus we encounter terms like *prakāśa, ābhāsa, vibhāsa, bimba-pratibimba* and of course *darpaṇa*. Only a *darpaṇa* is capable of *pratibimba*, a *darpaṇa* does not just contain the image but reflects it back and forth, and it is therefore that a *darpaṇa* embodies a movement. The *darpaṇa* becomes a beautiful example of *bhedābheda*, unity in difference. It is only a *darpaṇa* that can create an initial duality and yet maintain non-duality. Cognition according to Kāśmīr Śaivites consists of three components, *jñāna* or knowledge of the object of cognition, *smaraṇa* or remembrance and *apohana* or differentiation. It is in the concepts of *smaraṇa* and *apohana* that the Kāśmīr Śaivites part company from the Advaita Vedāntins and the Bauddhas. While the Vedāntins accept *smaraṇa* as a component of knowledge, the Bauddhas reject it. When it comes to *apohana* the Vedāntins pursue *apohana* by negation while the

Kāśmīr Śaivites carry out the process of *apohana* through affirmation. Thus *smaraṇa* and *apohana* become the hallmarks of the Kāśmīr Śaivite epistemology. Abhinavagupta emphasises the importance of *smaraṇa* when he says that "remembrance is unity in multiplicity. . . and therefore it is, that those who are well-versed in the *āgamas* hold that remembrance is like *cintāmaṇi*. "Remembrance itself, assuming the form of contemplation exposes your glory as *cintāmaṇi* does wealth."[77] Unlike the Bauddhas, Kāśmīr Śaivites insist that it is remembrance that refines cognition and leads to expansion of consciousness, and that without it consciousness would remain contracted. Multiple cognitions, or *pratyabhijñā*, which is the hallmark of Kāśmīr Śaivism cannot proceed unless there is the remembrance of the previous cognition. For it is Śiva "who strings in a regular order the multitude of gems, the objects, which lie heaped up in the treasury of his heart, on the string of remembrance".[78] It is *smaraṇa* or remembrance that along with *apohana śakti* or the power of differentiation, illumines an object of a former direct experience through perception. Without *smaraṇa* and *apohana*, perception would indeed be defective and limited, and therefore the twin epistemic acts of *smaraṇa* and *apohana* must be considered as part of perception itself, and an innate part of *kriyā*, and one that leads to a refined and clearer cognition. The entire edifice of *pratyabhijñā* rests on the foundational premise of *smaraṇa*, for without it repeated cognitions of the same object would lead to fragmented, rather than an integrated experience. This epistemic *smaraṇa* is the basis of the permanence of the self, the *aham*, the remembering of one's identity when one wakes up from sleep, and is the foundation of the *karma* doctrine, to which Kāśmīr Śaivism, like all other Indian Idealistic systems subscribes. The movement of the cognition *aham* to *aham idam*, is the expansion of *jñāna* through the process of *pratyabhijñā* and occurs only because of *smaraṇa*. It is *smaraṇa* that pierces the veil of ignorance, and does not lead to new knowledge but to a refined knowledge of the same object. The concept of remembrance features prominently as a literary device in classical literature. The forgetting and subsequent remembrance of king Duṣyanta in *Śākuntalam* is well-known. In the Śiva-Pārvatī myth it is Śiva who has momentarily forgotten that Pārvatī is none other than Dākṣāyaṇī or Satī, while Pārvatī has known all along of her previous birth and her destiny of being reunited with Śiva. Śiva's remembrance is brought about by the persona of Pārvatī, her penance, and her successful withstanding of the interrogation by Śiva in a disguise, events so vividly portrayed in the *Śiva Purāṇa* and in the *kāvyas*. In visual terms the concept of *smaraṇa* is brought out by the *darpaṇa* of Pārvatī, for it is the *darpaṇa* that leads Śiva to a second cognition of Pārvatī, a cognition in which he sees himself. The objection of the Buddhists to *smaraṇa* as a bonafide epistemic activity stems from their reluctance to recognise a permanent subject; for them there is no *jñātā* and no *kartā*, but just a series of momentary experiences, related to each other by the doctrine of *pratītyasamutpāda*. This concept of momentariness is obviously unacceptable to the Kāśmīr Śaivites.

Kāśmīr Śaivites posit a three-fold hierarchy in the cognitive process. The lowest order of cognition is *idam* which is the basic, dull, sleepy awareness of the insentient or *jaḍa*. At the other end is pure transcendental cognition, *parajñāna*, the cognition of a *ṛṣi*, which is not only universal in what it cognises but at the same time ineffable. This ultimate level of cognition is shared by all Idealistic systems, upholding as they do the Upaniṣadic Idealist doctrine. It is only in the terms they use in indicating the highest level of cognition that distinguishes one *darśana* from the other. The Vedāntin uses the term *parabrahman* while the Kāśmīr Śaivite call it *bhairava*. While agreeing on the ultimate, the two systems have fundamental and significant differences in the intermediate steps, differences that separate and therefore define the system. While lower orders of cognitions are a hindrance rather than a help for the Vedāntins, for the Kāśmīr Śaivite on the other hand the pure, universal I-consciousness must proceed from an initial, though impure, limited I-consciousness. For the Kāśmīr Śaivites this lower order of self-awareness is neither dispensable nor an illusion, as it is for the *Vedāntins*. This important difference is not mere esoteric hair-splitting but the foundation of an entire world-view which characterises the Kāśmīr Śaivite epistemology. It is because of its insistence on including rather than excluding, affirming rather than negating the objective world, that makes Kāśmīr Śaivism not only practical and worldly but at the same time endears itself to aesthetes and lends itself to be understood through the paradigm and the dynamics of the Śiva-Pārvatī marriage. For after an eventual *vedāntic* negation Śiva eventually affirms Pārvatī. While the term *suṣupta* describes the *vedāntic brahman*, it is *mithuna* that captures the *bhairava* of the Kāśmīr Śaivites. We are quick to point out that both *suṣupta* and *mithuna* are to be understood metaphorically by us as the right-handed *tāntrics*. Taking the terms literally would lead us to the left-handed path with its obvious ambiguity. It is the impure limited I-consciousness that Pārvatī urges Śiva to undertake, for she knows that without this intitial epistemic step, Śiva cannot reach the universal I-consciousness which he aspires. Pārvatī knows that Śiva cannot realise the *aham* without the *idam*. For, in entreating Śiva to take her as a bride Pārvatī's self-interest is limited, her greater concern is to break Śiva away from a solipsistic, self-enclosed, contracted state of mind which can only be devoid of final fruition. Śiva's penance and austerities towards self-knowledge, she rightly feels, would be futile, his efforts at self-realisation would remain unfulfilled, his cognitive efforts would not reach fruition, unless he is led away from his inward contemplation and taken towards an integral cognition which will include and embrace the world as exemplified by Pārvatī. It is this that stirs Pārvatī towards her liaison with Śiva, now romantic, now epistemic, a liaison that leads the *kavi* and the *śilpī* to inspired heights and the epistemologist to a state of wonder at the marked resemblance between the narrative on the one hand and the epistemology on the other.

Pārvatī as the embodiment of the perfect art object illustrates the fundamental epistemic principle that the object must arouse and woo the adept subject and that this arousal must stem from the perfection and inherent sensuousness of the object. Pārvatī is the perfect object and Śiva the consummate subject. The *Śiva Purāṇa*, through its narrative, emphasises the duality and the difference between Śiva and Pārvatī in many different ways and this is important not only to the devotee but even more to the epistemologist. The cognising subject and the object of cognition need to be different for an epistemic dialogue, and it is only when two disparate entities come together that the joy of that union is enhanced. Notice how the difference between Śiva and Pārvatī are brought out in this reprimand by the brahmin sage to Pārvatī when she admits of her love for Śiva:

> The great lord is bull-bannered. His body is smeared with ashes. His hair is matted. He is clad in the hide of a tiger. He has covered his body with the hide of an elephant. He holds the skull. Serpents twine around his limbs. Poison has left a mark on his neck. He eats even forbidden stuff. He has odd eyes and is definitely awful. His birth and pedigree cannot be traced. He is devoid of the enjoyment of a householder. He has ten arms. He is mostly naked and is ever accompanied by ghosts and goblins.
>
> What is the reason whereby you wish him to be your husband? O gentle lady where has your wisdom gone?
>
> A previous terrible activity of his has been heard by me. If you are interested in hearing I shall tell you.
>
> Dakṣa's daughter, the chaste lady Satī wooed Śiva as her husband. Fortunately their union was well-known.
>
> Satī was discarded by Dakṣa because she was the wife of the skull-bearing Śiva. Śiva too was overlooked in the sacrifice.
>
> On account of the insult Satī was infuriated and she discarded her dear life. Śiva too was abandoned by her.
>
> You are a jewel among women. Your father is the king of the mountain. Why do you crave for a husband like this and that too by means of a severe penance?
>
> Handing over a gold coin you wish to buy a piece of glass. Setting aside the pure sandal paste you wish to smear mud over your body.
>
> Unmindful of the sunlight you wish to have the light of the glowworm. Throwing away fine silk you wish to wear hide.
>
> Discarding the life at home you yearn for life in the forest. Lady, throwing away excellent treasure you wish a piece of iron in return.
>
> Leaving off the guardians of the quarters you run after Śiva. This is not well said. It is against the conventions of the world.

> Where you, with the eyes like petals of a lotus? Where this three-eyed creature, Śiva? You are moon-faced while Śiva is five-faced.
>
> On your head the divine plaited hair shines with glossy splendour like a serpent. But Śiva has only the matted hair to boast of.
>
> Sandal paste is applied on your body, while the ashes of the funeral pyre on that of Śiva. Where your silken garment and where the elephant hide of Śiva?
>
> Where the divine ornaments and where the serpents of Śiva? Where the deities around you and where Śiva fond of goblins and their oblations?
>
> Where the pleasing sound of tabor? Where his peculiar drum, the *ḍamaru*? Where the set of fine drums and the inauspicious sound of his horn?
>
> Where the inauspicious sound of double drum and where the sound of his throat. You two are mismatched.
>
> Where your necklace and where the garland of skulls that he wears? Where your rich divine unguent and where the ash from the funeral pyre that he has on his body?
>
> O divine lady, everything concerning you and Śiva, such as form and features is mutually discordant.[79]

Pārvatī's courtship and her marriage are already taking a different appearance viewed this way. The Śiva-Pārvatī dialogue of the Purāṇas and *mahākāvyas* becomes, to the perceptive epistemologist, no mere conversation between two mythic beings, nor the romantic dialogue of a *nāyaka* and a *nāyikā*, or the feigned admonishment of a sage to Pārvatī, but an unfolding of the epistemic dynamics of the Kāśmīr Śaivites. And by extension all plastic images of Śiva and Pārvatī do not just remain beautiful and sterile art objects but become artistic representations, pregnant with meaning, of the epistemic transactions between an adept cognising subject and a refined cognisable object, and ultimately of the joyously pulsating consciousness or *spandana* itself. And among the Śiva-Pārvatī images that of *ardhanārīśvara* is especially arresting, for it visually illustrates this throb of consciousness and as well the penultimate stage of perfect cognition, the dynamic harmony of the subject and the object.

A Portfolio of Siva-Parvati Images from the Author's Collection

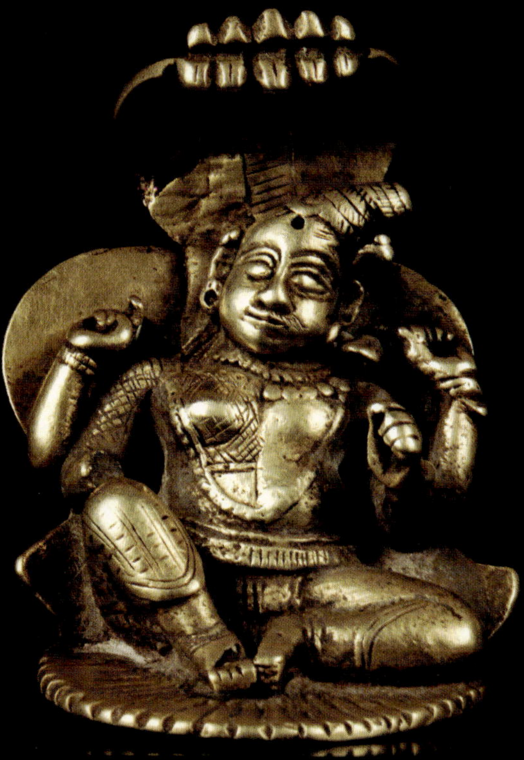

Vijaynagar, 16th Century

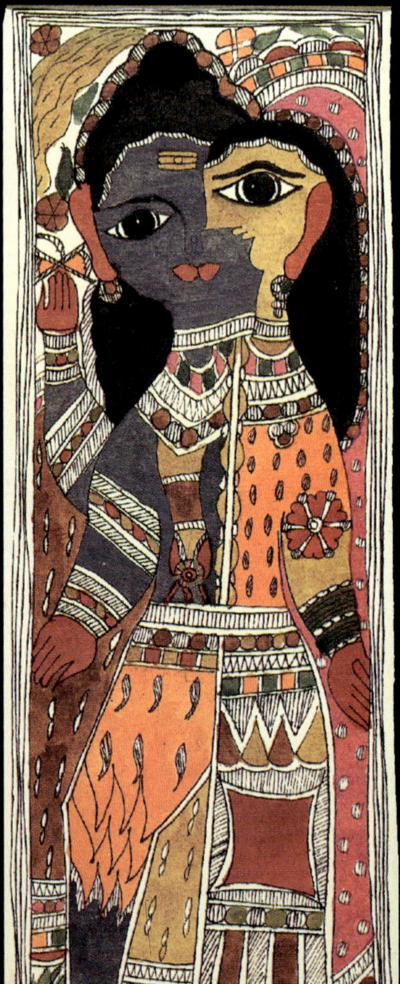

Madhubani, 20th Century

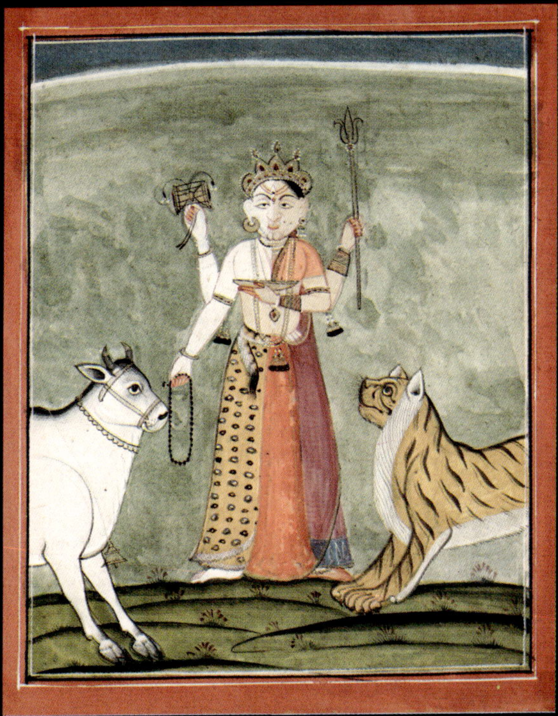

Chamba, Late 18th Century

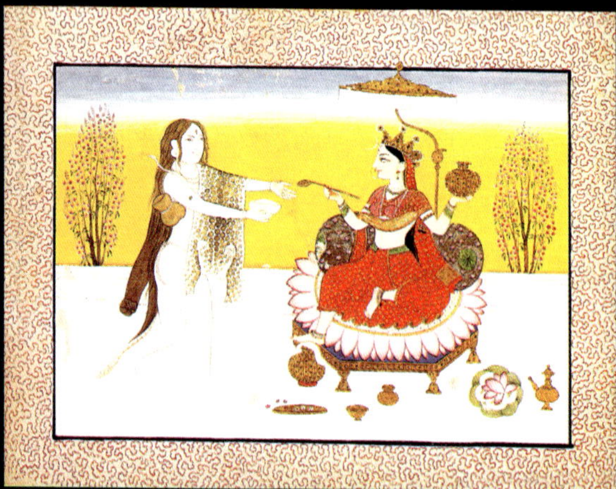

Kangra, 1820-40

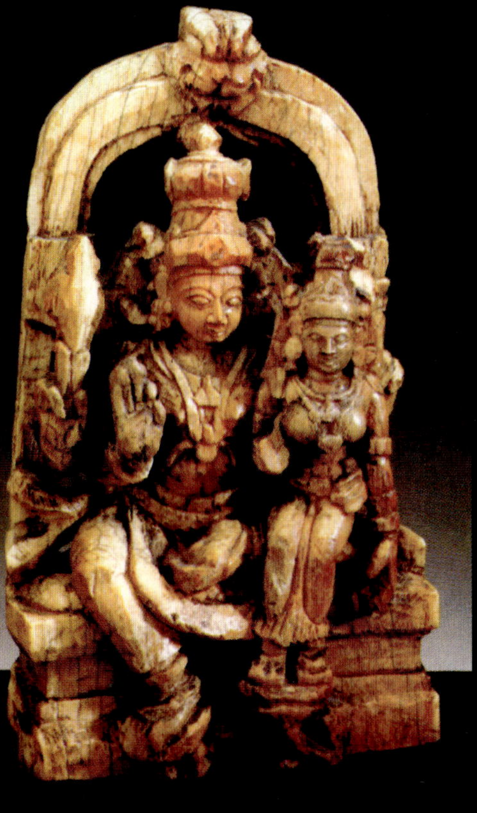

Maharashtra, 19th Century

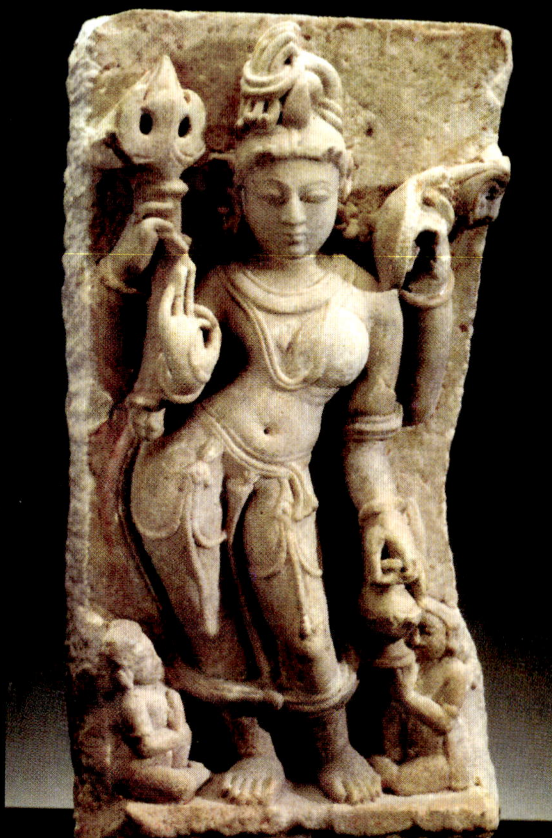

Central India, 10th Century

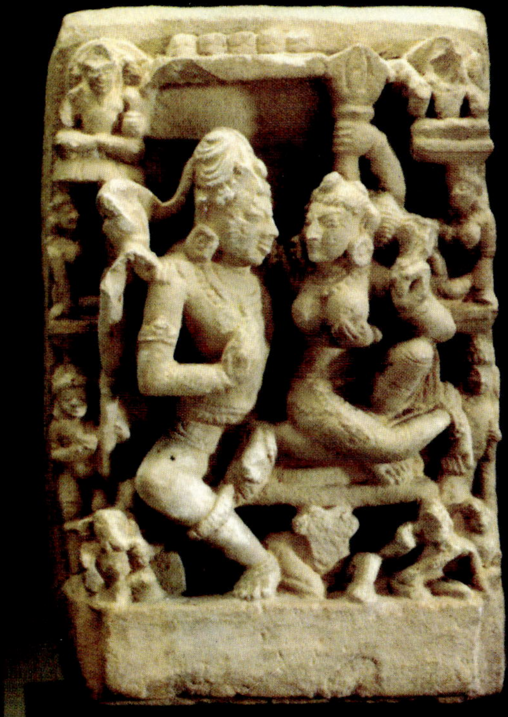

Central India, 10th Century

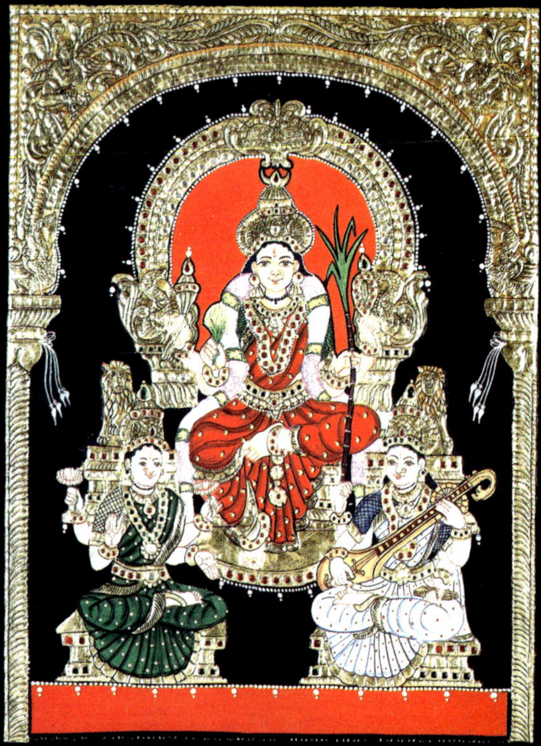

Tanjore, 20th Century

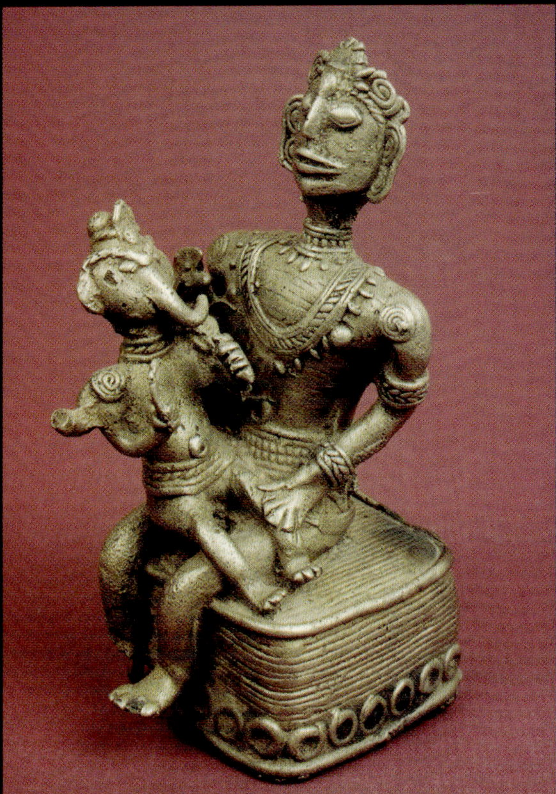

Bastar, 20th Century

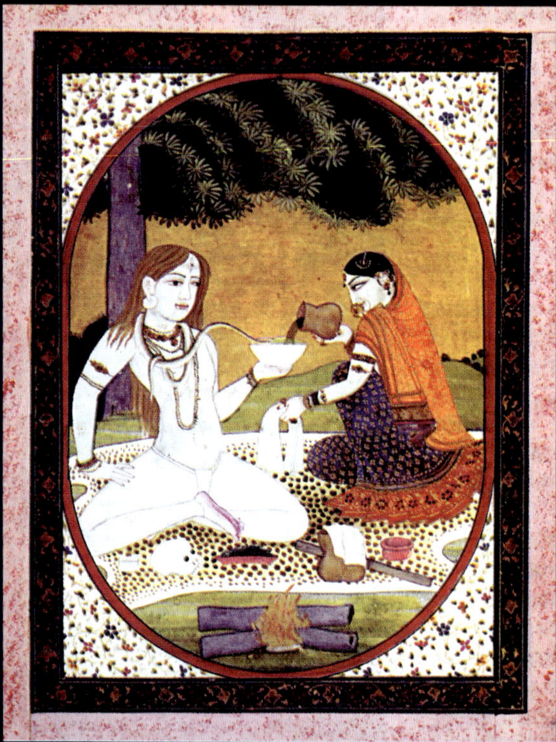

Gular, Late 18th Century

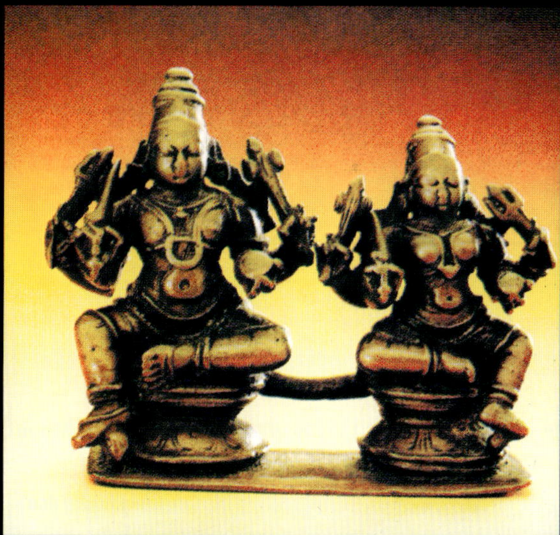

Vijaynagar, 16th Century

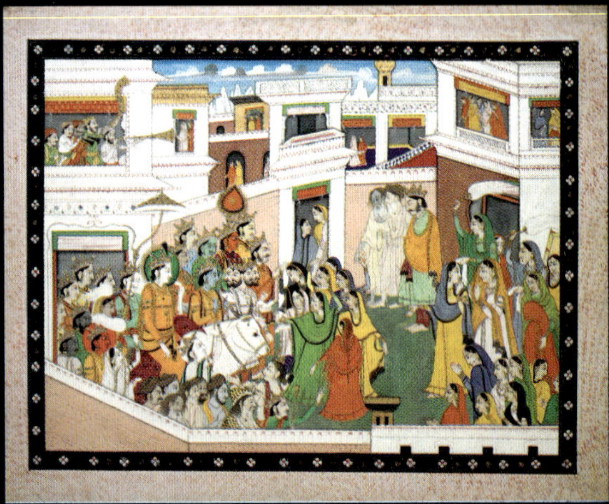

Kangra, 1820-30

But at this stage, let us turn our attention to the dynamics of the impure I-consciousness of the Kāśmīr Śaivite epistemology, which is the central plank of the doctrine and unique among the various *darśanas* of the Idealist systems.

The whole edifice of the Kāśmīr Śaivite epistemology is built on the initial, dualistic, impure, *aham-idam* I-consciousness, for it is this level of cognition that is pivotal to the understanding of the monistic Śaivite *yoga*, sometimes also referred to as the *yoga* of delight or the *yoga* of art. It is at this stage that the mystery of knowledge unfolds and the epistemic drama is enacted; it is at this stage of consciousness where subject and object encounter each other and experience *dvaita* initially and move into a higher phase of *advaita*, through an epistemic dialogue; for this is not a *nirvikalpa* but a *savikalpa* consciousness, not a state of conceptual emptiness but of conceptual richness, not a process of negation but of joyous affirmation, a stage of consciousness between outward gazing and inward looking, between outward expansion and inward contraction, a state of delightful vibration or *spandana*; it is at this stage that the apparently paradoxical reality of Śiva is confronted and it is this stage of Śiva's *dhyāna* which gives artistic expression to the various amorous Śiva-Pārvatī images. It is at this stage of *suṣumnā* that the throb of consciousness, the *spandana* of Śiva is experienced, not the wrathful and terrible Śiva as *bhairava* but an amorous Śiva, vibrating with joyous realisation, embracing the beautiful Pārvatī, an experience comparable to the aesthetic *dhyāna* of the *rasika* or the aesthete. It is the experience of not only *rasānanda* but *jagadānanda*, of bliss blossoming from a deliberate, penetrating, deeply meaningful aesthetic experience, of a state of bliss which converts, for Śiva, the entire world into an art object. It is the stage where the "tantric hero pushes outward into adventurous, spiritual exploration, into savouring and delighting the experience of so many varieties of the blissful *ekarasa*, the unitary taste of consciousness", only to exclaim joyously Śivo'ham![80] For Śiva-*rasikas* it is an invitation to participate, through the strikingly beautiful images of Śiva and Pārvatī, not only in the courtship and betrothal of Śiva and Pārvatī, but the wedding and the marital bliss that follows, not forgetting of course that Śiva and Pārvatī's arena is both the mythic Kailāsa as well as in our own being and in our own epistemic explorations. Not to immerse oneself in this sensuously rich and radiant event would be to plunge oneself into the sterility of the dark and insentient *jaḍa*, it would be to deny the dynamic play of *spanda* as it pulsates between Śiva and Pārvatī.

Self-reflection or reflexive consciousness is a fundamental feature of Kāśmīr Śaivism. Deep in his meditation Śiva is forced to pay attention to Pārvatī's presence and her beauty, for Pārvatī realises, committed as she is to *āgamic* epistemology, that Śiva's *nirvikalpa samādhi* will be abortive, for she knows that self-knowledge must take place through objective awareness and not through negation of the objective world. Pārvatī woos Śiva not only to take note of her presence by externalising his awareness, to undertake an *unmīlana samādhi*, a state of mind in which even when the eyes are open the external world appears as universal consciousness, but further to take her as a bride and finally to beget her a son. Pārvatī is not asking for a casual awareness on Śiva's part but a total and loving embrace, a *tanmayībhāva*, an epistemic *āliṅgana*; she asks that she play not the role of a courtesan but that of a bride; she asks not just for marriage but for its consummation with progeny. This is the Kāśmīr Śaivite meaning of self-reflection through objective awareness or *bhoga*.

It is because of Pārvatī *vimarśinī* that Śiva's consciousness is termed *prakāśavimarśamaya*. Consciousness in Kāśmīr Śaivism is not only *prakāśa* or luminous, but equally *vimarśa* or capable of self-reflection, not only *aham* or 'I' but *idam* or 'this', two aspects of consciousness as distinct as Śiva and Pārvatī, yet undivided as the *ardhanārīśvara*, as different and yet as tied as *śabda* is to its *artha*. In positing *vimarśa* as an integral part of consciousness the Kāśmīr Śaivites recognise the place of *unmīlana samādhi*, of opening a window to the objective world, persuading Śiva to abandon his solitary *tapas* and *nimīlana samādhi*, embrace Pārvatī and encouraging him to take Pārvatī as a bride. Pārvatī is not only a *yoginī* in her own right but a *vimarśinī*, initially ensuring *dvaitic* objective consciousness but leading it to *advaitic* subjective realisation through the epistemic processes of remembrance and the *rasa* of wonder. *Vimarśa* is an integral and indispensable part of self-knowledge and of sentiency itself and it is this *vimarśa* that becomes a defining feature of self-knowledge in Kāśmīr Śaivism. It is *vimarśa* that makes a quantum distinction between knowledge of "qualities such as white" and self-knowledge.[81] And it is *vimarśa* that "manifests the objects . . . on His clear mirror like self."[82] For self-knowledge is not just a contentless, passive, *aham* but a vibrant, content-rich biune unity of *aham-idam*, a state of Śiva-Śakti *sāmarasya*. We are further reminded that it is *vimarśa* that leads to *vikalpa* and "*vikalpa* owes its being to the awareness of another thing."[83] It is very clear that the Kāśmīr Śaivites make the pulsating *vimarśa* pivotal to their entire epistemology and it is this concept of *vimarśa* that distinguishes it from Śaṅkara's Advaita Vedānta. The *spandana* of *vimarśa* or the *idam*, makes the world of *nāma-rūpa* available to the cognising subject and ensures that cognition will be expansive, joyous, *savilakpa* and objective, enriching it not only with content but equally making the cognitive process pleasurable, a true *bhoga*. It has rightly been said that Śakti is the Śivahood of Śiva and Śiva alone is the Śaktihood of Śakti.[84] Śiva's persona is a biune unity arising out of the pulsation of *jñāna-śakti* and *kriyā-śakti*, driven by *icchā*, and true gnosis, or *śuddhavidyā* arises through a *spandana*, and through it a joyous coming together of the two.[85] Thus in *sūtra* after *sūtra*, the Kāśmīr Śaivites point to this fundamental concept of *śuddha-vikalpa*, a pulsating cognition, namely the amorous and joyous coming together of Śiva and Śakti, for the realisation of true knowledge or *śuddha-vidyā*. And for anyone steeped in the tradition it is hard to miss the striking similarity between this epistemology, characterised by a pulsation on the one hand, and the narrative of the marriage of Śiva and Pārvatī and the art it has inspired on the other. No other mythic marriage in this tradition bears this resemblance. While the wedding and celebrations that followed are of great interest to the aesthetician, what is of particular interest is the courtship of Śiva and Pārvatī. For it is during the courtship that Pārvatī works with sincerity and dedication to make her presence felt and move Śiva away from the inward, solipsistic and passive contemplation. Śiva is under the *vedāntic* illusion that *jñāna* devoid of *kriyā* is the key to bliss, whereas it is Pārvatī who recognises that it is *kriyā* that drives the *jñāna* experience to its highest reaches of fulfilment. Śiva's initial rejection and later acceptance of Pārvatī drives home this important epistemic principle of *kriyā* and *śakti*. The marriage of Śiva and Pārvatī also illustrates the concept of time. While Śiva is timeless, Śakti is the personification of time itself. For does not Pārvatī in her courtship come to Śiva again and again, illustrating temporality, while Śiva sits undisturbed, deep in his meditation, illustrating the concept of timelessness? For, the true realisation of timelessness can come through an experience of time, for, the movement between timelessness and time is a joyous *spandana*. Equally it stresses that *kriyā* is not just any activity but a refined activity directed to a befitting object, for Pārvatī is not only a *yoginī* in her own right but further subjects herself to severe austerities to purify herself even further. It is Pārvatī's mission to remove Śiva's delusion that she is just another person who can and should be ignored, but that in reality she is a part of him, only a throb of *spandana* away. It is her mission to convince Śiva that there can be no *jñāna* without *kriyā* and that *kriyā* leads to nothing but *jñāna*. It is she who makes him realise that without *icchā* and *kriyā* there can be no true *jñāna* and that it is only the twin processes of *icchā* and *kriyā* that leads the subject to a discovery of unity in diversity, *bheda-abheda*, and thereby providing objectivity to his inward contemplation and enriching his epistemic experience.[86] It is Pārvatī who restores integrality and wholeness to Śiva for through her persistent courtship she seems to ask Śiva a rhetorical question "how indeed can there be diversity in Him who is a single whole?"[87] For we are told that bondage and liberation, and unity amidst diversity, paradoxical as they are, are the very essence of Śiva.[88] Left to himself, and devoid of Pārvatī, Śiva alone in his inward contemplation, would not be in a position to solve these epistemic riddles of *jñāna* and *kriyā*. It is Pārvatī who emphasises that Śiva is the lord of the five-fold cosmic activities of *sṛṣṭi, sthiti, saṁhāra, apidhānam* and *anugraha,*[89] viz. creation, preservation, absorption, obscuration and revelation. The concept of *apidhāna* points to a certain primal epistemic amnesia and implies the basic human epistemic question "*ko'ham?*". Pārvatī takes it upon herself to remove Śiva's primal amnesia by first arousing Śiva and then, as it were, putting up a mirror in front of him. If *prakāśa* is given to amnesia, *vimarśa* is the process of awakening and remembrance; if *prakāśa* is the form, *vimarśa* is the essence; if *prakāśa* is the word, *vimarśa* is the meaning; if *prakāśa* is Śiva, *vimarśa* is Pārvatī. This is the constant refrain of Kāśmīr Śaivism, a refrain that reverberates throughout the Śiva-Pārvatī myth and equally in the art it inspires. Axiologically this Kāśmīr Śaivite epistemology leads to a joyous affirmation rather than a *vedāntic* negation of the world. It is this truly *advaitic* outlook that maintains a consistency between epistemology and axiology, between a world-view and social action, a consistency that Vedānta is unable to achieve as it advocates two realities, a provisional and an ultimate. The two realities of Vedānta involve negation whereas the multiple realities of Kāśmīr Śaivism are held together through joyous affirmation, for one level of reality is a mere reflection, an *ābhāsa*, of another.

Vimarśa, if unchecked, runs the risk of making cognition hedonistic and materialistic, of causing the *idam* to wander out of the grasp of the *aham*. The ability to preserve *advaita* while affirming *dvaita*, which is the foundational premise of Kāśmīr Śaivism, is best visualised by the artistic depiction of Śiva's *āliṅgana*, his loving embrace of Pārvatī. The left hand of Śiva lovingly and amorously embraces Pārvatī, as depicted in Śiva-Pārvatī images, and in that embrace is the preservation of *advaita* in the midst of *dvaita*, it is the embrace of Śiva that prevents the limitless expansion of Śiva's *śakti*, it is that amorous moment of subject-object consummation, of the *rasa* experience of a *rasika*, of unity in the midst of diversity, of *abheda* while affirming *bheda*, of *spandana* itself.[90] Śiva-Pārvatī iconography abounds in these amorous depictions of Śiva's *āliṅgana*. Pārvatī is shown either being lovingly held by Śiva or sitting on his knee; image after image, whether it be at the magnificent Khajuraho temples and especially in the Kandariya Mahadev temple, or in small Śiva shrines all over the country. Pārvatī has no standing or status of her own and is almost always seen in this beautiful, amorous, and visually pleasing *āliṅgana* with Śiva. Even when Pārvatī is absent in the composition, her presence is to be assumed by the outstretched left arm of Śiva suggesting an *āliṅgana.* A reticent Śiva, caught up in his nihilistic contemplation, passive, ignorant and indifferent to the world around him, has been aroused and awakened by Pārvatī. *Icchā* has led to *kriyā* in Śiva's encounter with Pārvatī. He now realises the romantic and epistemic value of Pārvatī and does not wish to let her go, lest he become solitary once again and therefore engages in an *āliṅgana*. Śiva has awakened to the pulse and the throb of *spandana*, he is now alert to the sound of the *ḍamaru* that he carries and which deep in his contemplation he had ignored. For isn't the *ḍamaru* of Śiva a visual paradigm of *spandana* itself, pulsing out time, heralding the biune unity of *jñāna* and *kriyā*, of Śiva and Pārvatī? And it was the *ḍamaru* that announced for the assembled guests at Śiva's wedding his ancestry. For ever watchful that the *advaitic* state not be tampered with and replaced by *dvaita*, now that he dances to the beat of his *ḍamaru*, Śiva ensures *advaita* through his *āliṅgana*. The divine couple and their amorous relationship mean many things to many people: to the devout an object of worship, to the artist an inspiration for artistic creation, to the aesthete a source of aesthetic contemplation and to the epistemologist a model of perfect cognition and therefore of aesthetic experience. And one role does not preclude another, for nothing prevents an aesthete from becoming a devotee and the devotee from turning his attention to the rich suggestions and nuances of epistemology in the images.

While the *āliṅgana* of Śiva is a visual depiction of *vimarśa*, it is the *darpaṇa* that beautifully emphasises the unique and all important concept of *pratyabhijñā*. The mirror in the hand of Pārvatī is not an object of feminine vanity, as some make it out to be, rather the mirror is so held, that Śiva can see his own face in it. Śiva's first cognition of Pārvatī, and his *āliṅgana*, is a lustful and outward epistemic step, an *unmīlana*, an expansion, ensuring that his attention and cognition is focused on Pārvatī rather than letting it expand limitlessly, but on second and subsequent cognitions Śiva sees the mirror in the hand of Pārvatī, in which he sees none other than himself. It is the *darpaṇa* that leads visual credence to the fundamental Kāśmīr Śaivite doctrine that "the objective status of the object is cognition itself."[91] *Pratyabhijñā*, or cognition through recognition, becomes an important and indispensable and pivotal component of *vimarśa*. It is *pratyabhijñā* that affirms that *vimarśa* is a *spandana*, a throb of cognition that pulses between the subject and the object. *Pratyabhijñā* gives legitimacy to *pratyakṣa* or perception as the highest *pramāṇa*, or mode of knowledge, and further illuminates the fact that in its highest reaches cognitive effort on the part of the subject is ultimately for the purpose of self-knowledge. *Pratyabhijñā* further illustrates the all important epistemic fact that *pramā, pramāṇa* and *prameya*, the perceiver, perception and the perceived are to be considered separate cognitive steps only for the purpose of an epistemic analysis, but in the end all three are part of the mass of *cidānanda* or blissful consciousness. While Śiva is the *pramā* and Pārvatī the *prameya*, their marriage understood in its wider epistemic sense becomes the *pramāṇa*. While the lordship of the perceiver is never in doubt in any system of philosophy, it is Kāśmīr Śaivism that insists that it is in understanding fully the true nature of the object that consciousness is truly understood. While affirming the Upaniṣadic dictum that knowledge is ultimately subjective it never loses sight of the object. Self-awareness, for Kāśmīr Śaivites, as it is for Śiva, can arise only from material cognition. Śiva cognises and understands Pārvatī in order to truly understand himself and what better aegis for this epistemic activity than a joyous marriage. This pivotal fact of Kāśmīr Śaivite epistemology is brought out by the *darpaṇa* in the hand of Pārvatī. While the strikingly beautiful image of the *ardhanārīśvara* displays the *darpaṇa*, the narrative of the Śiva-Pārvatī marriage, which of course does not talk of a mirror, makes it clear that Pārvatī wishes that Śiva treat her as if she holds a mirror, and see himself in that mirror. In the narrative of the Śiva-Pārvatī marriage the mirror of Pārvatī is implied but cannot be described. The various actions of Pārvatī leave little doubt that she wishes to become, as it were, a mirror to Śiva. If *vimarśa* through *unmīlana*, cognitively includes the outside world in consciousness, *pratyabhijñā* or *nimīlana*, ensures that this cognition does not become hedonistic but leads to a restful self-awareness. *Pratyabhijñā* is the logical outcome of the *spandana* of *vimarśa*. The mirror of Pārvatī ensures that the cognition of Śiva turns back upon itself, becomes reflexive, assuring that this objective cognition leads ultimately to self-awareness, for Śiva in his second and subsequent cognitions sees none other than himself in the mirror. In reflecting the image back to its source it is the mirror of Pārvatī that ensures that Śiva, who is the subject, remains the driving force of the epistemic process. The mirror also ensures that the object is upheld and given an epistemic bonafides and not dismissed as an illusion or unimportant, and further that there is a *spandana* or continuity of the pulsation between the subject and the object. Throughout the epistemic dialogue between Śiva and Pārvatī the biune unity of the subject and the object is affirmed, for it is a unity born of affirmation and not negation, it is a unity in the midst of diversity, it is a unity born of the joy of the romantic togetherness of Śiva and Pārvatī. It is Pārvatī's mirror that ensures that Śiva's *āliṅgana* does not become merely materialistic and hedonistic; it instead assures that this *āliṅgana* is spiritual and turned inwards, that the initial and dualistic cognition of the object is converted to *advaitic* and larger self-awareness, that Śiva's cognition of Pārvatī remains tied to Śiva, as *artha* is to the *śabda*. If the *āliṅgana* of Śiva gives epistemic legitimacy to the objectivity of Pārvatī, giving it an epistemic bonafides, and not discarding it as mere illusion, it is the mirror that ensures that Śiva himself is the resting point of that cognition, meeting the Idealistic premise. This, to and fro movement of consciousness, from the subject to the object and back to the subject, the *spandana* or *sphurattā* of Śiva, constitutes the essence of *pratyabhijñā*. Lest it be forgotten, amidst the celebration of the Śiva-Pārvatī marriage, that while the aesthete is partaking of the celebrations, through the artistic depictions, the epistemologist is equally interested in the cognitive process at work in the aesthete. The aesthete, like Śiva, must hold the different cognitions and unite them on "the one wall of the universal light of consciousness"[92] for this is what provides the continuity, the stability and the resting point of the cognitive process. The ***Kramasūtra*** says that "just as fire set ablaze consumes the fuel even one should consume the objects of sense which act like fetters."[93] Sensual joyous affirmation through *kriyā* remains the foundational principle of Kāśmīr Śaivism, and an integral part of *jñāna*. The key word here is "*bhakṣayet*", consuming as it were with relish, converting the process into an aesthetic rather than a volitional activity, into an activity to be relished and not shunned, and not ignoring or negating it as mere illusion, as the *vedāntins* would. Utpaladeva gives primacy to sensual enrichment when he says "let my senses become full, pure, devoted and strong."[94] The ***Svacchanda Tantra*** calls the process "resting of the external object in the essential nature of the knower."[95] For exponents of the *pratyabhijñā*, or the Trika *darśana*, maintain unequivocally, that the *ātman* is both immanent in the universe and transcends it, that the universe is not only inherent but instrumental in Śiva's self-awareness.[96] This dual relationship of immanence as well as transcendence comes about not by the cognitive efforts of the subject alone but is equally made possible by the excellence and purity of the object, in other words there is a happy marriage of the consummate subject and the perfect object, of Śiva and Pārvatī. In aesthetic terms the subject has not only to be a trained aesthete but equally that the art object be a fit object of aesthetic contemplation. No wonder then that the wedding and the marriage of Śiva and Pārvatī is celebrated with such rejoicing, not only by poets such as Kālidāsa and *śilpīs* of the past as in temples of Khajuraho, but by devotees even today, as witnessed at the Mīnākṣī temple in Tamil Nadu. Epistemically the celebration of the wedding of Śiva and Pārvatī is nothing other than the affirmation of the object and the coming together of that object with the cognising subject, thereby celebrating the *advaita* of joyous affirmation.

Kālidāsa spares no words in describing the festivities and joy in the Himalayan town of Oṣadhiprastha as they prepare for the wedding of Śiva and Pārvatī:

> "The high roads of the city were strewn with heavenly flowers, with rows of silken flags, and with the brilliant golden

outer gates it was as if heaven was transplanted."[97]

The epistemic value and therefore immanence of the objective world is beautifully brought out not only by the *āliṅgana* of Śiva which ensures that once Pārvatī has been cognised she is not lost, but equally by the attributes of Pārvatī, who is not only sensuously desirable but intellectually refined. Equally the joyousness of the wedding speaks of the immanence, in which both the bride and the groom, their families and relatives, participate with enthusiasm and celebration. This is not ordinary wedding but that of the daughter of Parvata and Menā, where the whole town of Oṣadhiprastha turn out to participate in the celebrations. The transcendence on the other hand is illustrated by the *darpaṇa* of Pārvatī which unlike a *madanikā-darpaṇa*, ensures that Śiva, and not Pārvatī, sees himself in that mirror. If Pārvatī were not the consummate object and were she not able to reflect the cognitive process back to Śiva through her mirror, the tandem function of immanence and transcendence would not be possible. Pārvatī is confident and poised, self-assured in the knowledge of her own physical charm and aware of her destiny that she was born to marry none other than Śiva. Of her beauty Kālidāsa has said that "she was created by the Creator of the universe with great effort, as if with a desire to see all beauty combined in one form."[98] And none other than Śaṅkara in his ***Saundaryalaharī*** undertakes a description of her beauty in the traditional style of starting with the head and going down to the foot.[99] Pārvatī is the embodiment and the epitomy of perfect sensual beauty in the Indian tradition.

And having married him she is committed to the success and happiness of the marriage. Like a devoted wife it is her mission to serve and satisfy her husband and cater to all his needs. For she is even prepared to serve Śiva's snake as is seen in a Pahāḍī miniature. The ***Śiva Purāṇa*** celebrates the romance of Śiva and Pārvatī thus:

> When Śiva returned to Kailāsa the joyful *gaṇas* made all arrangements for his happiness. When Śiva returned to Kailāsa there was great jubilation there. The gods returned to their realms with their mind full of joy. Then taking Pārvatī, the

daughter of the mountain with Him, Śiva, the great Lord, went to a delightful brilliant isolated place.

Making a wonderful bed conducive to good sexual pleasure, rendered smooth and fragrant with flowers and sandal paste and auspiciously supplemented with objects of enjoyment, lord Śiva, the bestower of honour indulged in dalliance with Pārvatī for a thousand years of god.

In that divine sport at the mere contact with Pārvatī, Śiva lapsed into unconsciousness. She too lapsed into unconsciousness due to contact with Śiva. She neither knew the day nor night.

When Śiva following the worldly way began his enjoyment of pleasures, O sinless one, a great length of time passed by as though it was a mere moment in their awareness.[100]

Even *śṛṅgāra-rasa kāvyas* such as the Bhānudatta's ***Rasamañjarī*** celebrate the romance of Śiva and Pārvatī in these lines spoken by Pārvatī to Śiva in their love play:

"Surrender unto me my necklace, which you have today stolen during our game of dice. (It is no use denying the theft). I cannot accept your swearing by the holy Gaṅgā which you carry on your head, nor your swearing by the holy fire which you hold in your eyes, nor your swearing by the snakes which you wear on your body."[101]

Kālidāsa's final canto in his ***Kumārasaṁbhava*** is devoted entirely to the dalliance of Śiva and Pārvatī and he surpasses even the ***Śiva Purāṇa*** in describing with romantic lyricism the amorous relationship between the two:

After the wedding ceremony, as the daughter of the lord of the mountains experienced fear mixed with love towards Śiva, he enjoyed thrilling pleasure which heightened his desire. 8.1

When her lover full of curiosity feigned to be asleep Pārvatī turned her eyes towards his face, but as he smilingly opened his eyes she closed hers as if (they had been) struck by lightning. 8.3

Trembling, she obstructed the hand of Śaṅkara as it was placed near the region of her navel; but her garment of its own accord had its tying knot completely loosened. 8.4

> In private, with her garment taken off, she closed Śiva's (two) eyes with her two palms; but as his (third) eye on his forehead continued looking, she had her efforts foiled and became helpless. 8.7
>
> Dear to Śiva was the union with his bride although it obstructed passion, and in which response was difficult to obtain, there being no offering of the lower lip (on her part) while kissing, while her hands hung loose when very firmly embraced. 8.8
>
> And while observing in a mirror (the marks of) enjoyment when she saw immediately behind her own reflection that of her lover seated at the back—what was it that she did not do in shame? 8.11
>
> After a few days, Śiva, with great difficulty caused his beloved to be reconciled to (love sport). Having known the taste of love she gradually abandoned her perverseness towards enjoyment. 8.13
>
> In a few days, only their affection for each other grew strong, the (affection) which was manifested by their gestures, in which displeasure was not to be seen, which was full of pleasing talk, and which could not tolerate separation even for a moment. 8.15
>
> The skill proper for young ladies, which she learnt when she became the disciple in private of Śiva, who taught her enjoyment, that same (skill) she offered to him by way of teacher's remuneration. 8.17
>
> Being closely clasped round his neck by the tender arms of Pārvatī as she was frightened at the roar of Rāvaṇa, the father of the universe enjoyed bright moonlight on the mountain of Kubera (Kailāsa). 8.24
>
> While Śiva was sporting there, treating day and night both equally, he passed a hundred and fifty seasons as though it was one night. He did not lose his thirst for amorous pleasures as the fire inside the ocean (is never satiated) with its rolling waters. 8.91.[102]

And further through her mirror Pārvatī ensures that Śiva's transcendence is not compromised by the process of *unmīlana*. Pārvatī brings about this *unmīlana* or an expansion of Śiva's cognition at the risk of introducing an initial duality in the cognitive process, in keeping with the *pratyabhijñā* view, that "those who are attached to the limited as the Self do not reach the highest stage of Śiva,"[103] but at the same time ensures a *nimīlana* or introversion through her mirror, so that the cognition rests in Śiva's self-awareness. It is Pārvatī that creates the *spandana* between *unmīlana* and *nimīlana*, between Śiva's awareness of the world around and self-awareness. That self-awareness which has been brought about by the mirror, is a *pratimīlana* or a coming together of *unmīlana* (expansion) and *nimīlana* (introversion) in which all traces of difference have vanished.[104] For this state of *pratimīlana* is nothing other than *Śiva-śakti-sāmarasya*, the undifferentiated and joyous state of consciousness, a state of consciousness that is fully awakened and enlarged, in which subject-object duality ceases for ever, where there is a shattering of the initial illusion of duality[105] and of time itself, a state represented by the image of *ardhanārīśvara*. The *darpaṇa* becomes not just a *badhra* in the hands of a deity, not just another attribute of a mythic image, but a statement of the very reason of the togetherness of Śiva and Pārvatī. It is the *darpaṇa* that ensures that "the knower and the known are one and the same"[106] and thus leads to a state of delight. It is only in that state of delight that one can exclaim that one has understood "the quintessence of the union of Śiva and śakti".[107] It is only in the state of *śiva-śakti-sāmarasya* that Śiva's egoistic, limited, self-absorption has been shattered and born into a larger self-awareness through the *rasa* of wonder. As Dyczkowski rightly points out, "When this false identification is overcome, consciousness which formerly seemed contracted, now presents itself in its true fully expanded (*vikasita*) form. The individual ego merges in the pervasive universal ego, just as the space in the broken jar merges with the space around it."[108] It is worth repeating that it is the state of delight and wonder that Śiva experiences from cognising Pārvatī that assures Śiva an expansion of his consciousness, for it is this delight that lets the subject "distinguish between the particular and generic vibration of consciousness."[109] The particular vibration or *viśeṣa-spanda* is analogous to the *cittavṛtti* of Patañjali and must not be confused with the universal vibration or *sāmānya-spanda*; it is only the latter that leads to the pure 'I'-consciousness. We can only affirm with Dyczkowski when he says that "*Spanda* converts the cold, impersonal absolute of monistic Vedānta of Śaṅkara into the warm, worshipful absolute of Kāśmīr Śaivism."[110] It has rightly been said that if Śiva be the *upeya, spanda* is the *upāya*.

It is important to point out that the *darpaṇa* represents the intermediate stage, a gap between *unmīlana* and *nimīlana*, and this mid-cognitive stage is given considerable importance not only by Kāśmīr Śaivites but even by Patañjali in his ***Yogasūtras.*** Abhinavagupta states that real knowledge is the knowledge one derives by the contemplation that occurs between two cognitions,[111] for it is in the gap between two cognitions that there is the realization of pure consciousness in all its intensity.[112] It becomes clear that Kāśmīr Śaivism, in keeping with its Idealistic credo, also gives pride of place to *nirvikalpa jñāna*, or non-cognitive awareness, but unlike Advaita Vedānta is not prepared to sacrifice the initial *savikalpa jñāna* or cognitive knowledge. Relating this to the Śiva-Pārvatī myth, Śiva has multiple cognitions of Pārvatī, now a fleeting glimpse, now a lustful longing of Pārvatī, now majestic as she discourses with Śiva and now vulnerable as she is subjected to an interrogation by Śiva in his disguise as an old man. It is the *darpaṇa* of the *ardhanārīśvara*, in which is reflected the image of Śiva, between two cognitions, that is the *madhya-bhāva*, for Śiva is indeed the eternal subject, the uninterrupted consciousness upon which the cognitive dialogue with Pārvatī takes place. It is the *darpaṇa* that creates the *spandana*, the vibration between Śakti and Śiva. As Dyczkowski says, "There is a movement (*spanda*) of awareness from one to the other as Śiva becomes Śakti and Śakti becomes Śiva. They are reflected within one another like two mirrors facing each other."[113] Śiva and Śakti are the divine couple, *yamala*, and *spanda* is the pulsation between the two. It is a case of not just *bimba* but *bimba-pratibimba*. However, while Śiva is the ground of all being it is Pārvatī that makes it possible for Śiva to have self-awareness through *spanda*, once again emphasising that *savikalpa jñāna* is both instrumental and inherent in *nirvikalpa jñāna*. And that is why Kāśmīr Śaivites stress that *jñāna* is self-awareness and that it can only result from *kriyā* or the *spandana* of cognitive activity. Kāśmīr Śaivism complies with the Upaniṣadic position when it postulates that complete self-awareness in the end leads to stillness.[114]

The all important concept of *madhya-bhāva* ties in with the equally fundamental concept of *kāla* or time. Abhinavagupta states that "the essence of time consists in the experience of successive appearance and disappearance of objects."[115] Pārvatī is time personified and Śiva the personification of timelessness. While Pārvatī comes and goes, now triumphant and now frustrated, to and from Kailāsa, Śiva meditates; while Pārvatī is the essence of movement, Śiva is the essence of stillness; while Pārvatī is *vimarśa*, Śiva is *prakāśa*; while Pārvatī is the *artha*, Śiva is the *śabda*; while Pārvatī is the vowel, Śiva the consonant; while Śiva is timelessness, Pārvatī is time. Abhinavagupta reminds us that "time is only a thought-construct"[116] and by the same token we can therefore say that all thought-constructs abide in time, appearing unbroken and continuous on the surface, but indeed as separate as a "hundred flowers and buds pierced together" in a garland.[117] This understanding of time is essential for not only does it shed light on the epistemic nature of objective phenomena or *prameya* which abide in time, but shows how these phenomena are different from subjective realisation or *pramā* which is the abode of timelessness. Defined by time, Pārvatī initially fails to arouse Śiva who abides in timelessness, for on the surface the two, time and timelessness, are incompatible, unlikely marriage partners. Were it not for the *darpaṇa*, neither time nor timelessness, nor *savikapla* and *nirvikalpa jñāna*, would be complimentary to each other. It is the *darpaṇa* that creates a happy marriage, the perfect state of knowledge, the state of biune unity, created by joyous affirmation and not nihilistic negation. The ***Spandakārikā*** expresses the same idea when it states: "When the *yogī* desirous of seeing, stands fixed, covering all objects with the light of his consciousness, he experiences the entire objective world in himself, in that state (of realisation) what is the use of words?[118] It is Pārvatī that breaks Śiva out of his limited consciousness into a state of universal consciousness, giving him "full acquisition of mastery over the collective whole of *śaktis*".[119] It is she who leads

Śiva into a state of *śuddha-vidyā*, a state of knowledge that moves from "*aham*" to "*aham idam*" and ultimately to "*aham eva sarvam*".[120] Pārvatī no longer remains a sensuous bride but becomes the embodiment of knowledge itself, for as the ***Śiva Sūtras*** says "she is the highest *vidyā*".[121] If "*aham*" is the voice of the unmarried Śiva, "*aham idam*" is the song of the amorous togetherness of Śiva and Pārvatī, "*aham eva sarvam*" is the hymn of the fully realised Śiva. Pārvatī, is no mere bride, or an object of sensuous beauty but an embodiment of everything that can be objectified and fit to be cognised. In endearing herself to Śiva through her romantic transaction Pārvatī is ensuring that she become the universal object incorporating into herself the objective world. Without the cognition of Pārvatī, Śiva's awareness would stay limited to a mere passive and somnolent "*aham*". It is she who exalts Śiva's mind and makes it ready for the final restful and wondrous realisation. Tagore has put it beautifully when he says:

> This principle of unity is the mystery of all mysteries. The existence of a duality at once raises a question in our minds, and we seek its solution in the One. When at last we find a relation between these two, and thereby see them as one in essence, we feel that we have come to the truth. And then we give utterance to this most startling of all paradoxes, that the One appears as many, that appearance is the opposite of truth and yet is inseparably related to it.[122]

The ***Vijñānabhairava*** has prescribed in no uncertain terms that the mind should initially be joyous before it can undertake realisation, that this joyousness is the pre-requisite for a higher epistemic step.[123] It becomes clear that the joyous marriage of Śiva and Pārvatī no longer remains a social event in the realm of myth, neither an emotional episode in the life of mythic beings, but an essential step in the growth of knowledge and the subsequent expansion of consciousness, illustrating the all-important concept of *tuṣṭi* or exultation. It is this exultation that leads to the expansion of cognition from "*aham*" to "*aham idam*" and finally to "*aham eva sarvam*". This expansion through exultation fully explains the meaning of the term *kriyā* and leaves no doubt that knowledge, in the Kāśmīr Śaivite epistemology, as opposed to the epistemology of Advaita Vedānta, is not passive but active. As Dyczkowski rightly points out that "knowledge turns into action and action leads to knowledge."[124] *Jñāna* cannot remain passive or limited but is driven by the exulted mind until it is fully universalized and in this process the knowledge episode moves from the perception of the outer form to the realisation of the inner nature, from *savikalpa* to *nirvikalpa*, from cognition to non-cognitive restful awareness or *viśrānti*. The *darpaṇa* of Pārvatī provides the epistemic gap in the all-important transition from *savikalpa* to *nirvikalpa jñāna*. Śiva's cognition in the mirror is not mere perception on his part but is equally an aesthetic experience and this needs to be understood and emphasised. When Śiva's initial cognition of Pārvatī is transformed through the mirror, into a cognition of none other than himself, he is wonderstruck and amazed, and experiences the *bhāva* of *adbhuta*, and it is this that exults his mind. For truly has it been said, the stages and the unfoldment of *yoga* are indeed a wonder.[125] While the dialogue and romance of Śiva and Pārvatī contains *śṛṅgāra rasa*, the more predominant *rasa* is one of *adbhuta*. What was once an irritant in Śiva's meditation has led to Śiva's self-awareness, what was once seen as a dualistic appearance is seen as firmly tied to himself. This creates a sense of wonder and excitement in Śiva. For the Kāśmīr Śaivites the stages of the expansion of consciousness are wondrous indeed and a source of unmitigated and unbounded joy. For, to see oneself unexpectedly, and that too through another, whom one has initially considered alien, is indeed a cause of amazement and wonder. Does not a child feel amazed when he looks over a still lake only to see his own image on the surface of the water, or a person feels excited when he meets a long lost friend? The mirror then becomes the agent of providing Śiva with a *rasa* experience, and it is the *adbhuta rasa* that leads to an expansion of his consciousness from *aham* to *aham eva sarvam*. Śiva is truly amazed that he is nothing other than Pārvatī and Pārvatī nothing other than he, leading to a pulsing rhythm of consciousness, from *bimba* to *pratibimba*. Even the *rasika* who participates in the marriage of Śiva and Pārvatī as an aesthete "experiences the birth of a higher level of consciousness within himself."[126] The fundamental reason for Śiva's amazement is the transformation of *dvaita* into *advaita*, of an initial dualistic cognition into a unitary cognition, of having realised what one had momentarily forgotten. Without the initial duality, and therefore an epistemic amnesia, the realisation of *tādātmya* or oneness, would have no excitement. As the ***Śiva Sūtra*** rightly points out "(Śiva) relishes the aesthetic delight born of objectivity by penetrating into his true nature which is the mass of consciousness."[127] The *rasa* doctrine, in no uncertain terms, speaks of the process of *sādhāraṇīkaraṇa* or universalisation, as an essential part of the *rasa* experience. It is the *rasa* experience that converts the particular into the universal, for without this expansion of consciousness, through the process of *spanda*, Śiva would still be limited to the finite, and less than joyous, experience of *aham*. It is for this reason that Pārvatī entreats Śiva to break out of his self-imposed solitude and take her on as a bride, and epistemologically this is the essence of the Śiva-Pārvatī marriage. Epistemologically the expansion of Śiva's knowledge from *aham* to *aham eva sarvam* points to the strength of *pratyabhijñā* as an epistemic tool as it leads the subject from knowledge to greater knowledge through the process of repeated cognitions and within the cognitive process it points to the value of perception as a cognitive process. Kāśmīr Śaivite epistemology leaves little doubt that sensory perception alone is the door to higher knowledge. Not only is the value of perception as a *pramāṇa par excellence* affirmed in this system, but the bliss that the perception has created points to the all important fact that consciousness cannot rest within itself, passive, somnolent and inward, but must self-reflect through objective awareness. It is the *spanda* of consciousness that alone can create self-reflection and therefore self-knowledge. The departure from Śaṅkara's epistemic position is too obvious to be repeated. For it is the perception of Pārvatī, through the romance and excitement and in particular of the mirror that has caused Śiva to cognise himself and it is that very perception that causes the *adbhuta rasa* experience.

An important part of the *adbhuta rasa* experience, that takes place because of the mirror in the hand of Pārvatī, is not only the wonder of the expansion of awareness but also remembering what was once forgotten, a correction of epistemic amnesia. Śiva's initial neglect of Pārvatī is born out of amnesia, an amnesia that has clouded his faculties from the tragic death of Satī. For did he not carry Satī's dead and charred body from Dakṣa's *yajña* and perform the *tāṇḍava bhairava*? The *tāṇḍava* that shook the three worlds has left Śiva in a state of amnesia and it is Pārvatī's task to draw him out of that state. For Satī, unlike Śiva, knows that she will return once again to be Śiva's wife. And even as Pārvatī is born she fully remembers the *saṅkalpa* that she has made in a previous birth. While ordinary mortals forget their *saṁskāras* at birth, Pārvatī who is a born *yoginī* suffers from no such amnesia. The cognition of Pārvatī by Śiva leads to his wonderment in two distinct ways. Firstly there is the joy of finding Satī, now in the form of Pārvatī, that shakes him out of his silent despair. But equally importantly, Śiva is wonderstruck by the second and subsequent cognition of Pārvatī that reveals the mirror through which Śiva sees himself. It is as it were Śiva has participated in a magical performance. Both the correction of amnesia and the expansion of consciousness is an aesthetic experience, an experience of *adbhuta rasa*. It is this kind of cognition that underscores the Kāśmīr Śaivite position that knowledge of ultimate reality is a step ladder process proceeding step by step, from joy to greater joy, but that the penultimate step requires a leap, a leap produced by the thrill and unbounded joy of the expansion of consciousness.[128] It is important to point out that only in the Śiva-Śakti *sāmarasya* state does Śiva experience his expanded universalised consciousness, and in that state Pārvatī is not just instrumental but inherent. Abhinavagupta stresses that the universal I-consciousness is "the most essential characteristic of the light of consciousness,"[129] and that "in this pure universalised state of consciousness objects shine as one with the subject, exactly in the manner in which a city shines in a mirror."[130] It is because of the *adbhuta-rasa* arising from the cognitive activity that one can say that *brahma-jñāna* is truly an aesthetic experience and that epistemology and aesthetics are twin brothers. The ***Śvetāśvatara Upaniṣad*** echoes a similar sentiment when it says: "Even as a mirror stained by dust shines brilliantly when it has been cleansed; So the embodied one, on seeing the nature of the Self, becomes unitary, his end attained and from sorrow freed."[131] And equally the ***Taittirīya Upaniṣad*** says: "*raso vai saḥ. hyevāyaṁ labdhvā ānandī bhavati.*" [132] The sense of excitement or heightened awareness in the state of *adbhuta-rasa* is an essential part of the experience of higher knowledge. The ***Spanda Kārikā*** clearly states that "the *spanda* principle is firmly established when a person is exasperated, enraged or is overjoyed."[133] It is during the intense emotionally exulted state of the mind, as is Śiva in his romantic involvement with Pārvatī, that one approaches the state of perfect knowledge.[134] The Kāśmīr Śaivites emphasise the excitement and thrill as a necessary prelude in the process of knowledge, comparing it to the joy of seeing a friend after a long time.[135] In our paradigm of the marriage of Śiva and Pārvatī, it is the thrill and excitement that Śiva experiences from the *darpaṇa* of Pārvatī that becomes the prelude and a stepping stone for ultimate knowledge.

Pārvatī has occasioned an aesthetic experience in Śiva and by this act becomes the embodiment of a perfect art object. The entire *rasa* doctrine was developed in the ambience of *nāṭya* and *kāvya*, by aestheticians such as Bharata and Abhinavagupta and the many that came in between and beyond. The various aesthetic theories took their stand on *nāṭya* and *kāvya* as art objects. In the marriage of Śiva and Pārvatī it is Pārvatī that becomes the art object and the *darpaṇa* the turning point of the entire cognitive experience of Śiva. Śiva's cognition satisfies the twin concepts of *tanmayī-bhāva* and *sādhāraṇikaraṇa* so essential for a *rasa* experience. While Pārvatī's one pointed devotion to Śiva finally manages to break Śiva out of his inward and self-effacing contemplation and lead him to *tanmayī-bhāva*, it is the mirror that leads to the process of *sādhāraṇīkaraṇa* and universalisation of Śiva's consciousness. The marriage of Śiva and Pārvatī not only provides a paradigm for *pratyabhijñā* but is a beautiful illustration of the *rasa* doctrine as well.

The *adbhuta-rasa* experienced by Śiva, and occasioned by the *darpaṇa*, is an epistemic step of considerable importance and one that needs to be emphasised. The sentiment of *vismaya* which is an essential ingredient of aesthetic experience and which is variously called *saṁvega*, aesthetic shock, aesthetic thrill and aesthetic arrest, points to the stillness that follows one pulse of the throb of *spandana*, for in that moment of amazement the mind is brought to a stillness and wanders no more, the repeated cognitions have brought fruit and the mind is ready to reap the harvest and turns inward in amazement and satisfaction, in rest and solitude and in full realisation of its fullness. The mind is indeed in a state of *citta-vṛtti-nirodha* as prescribed by Patañjali[136] and we are justified in calling the Śiva-Pārvatī-vivāha a *yoga*, both for Śiva and those of us who choose to undertake a contemplation of that mythic event. The ***Śiva Sūtras*** rightly says: "the senses of the *yogī* convert the world drama into a pleasing revelation of the true inner self, and create an aesthetic rapture in which any sense of duality has disappeared."[137] The entire cognitive process and the various steps within it is a wondrous experience for Śiva, for has not the ***Śiva Sūtras*** said that the unfoldment of the stages of *yoga* are wondrous?[138] The concept of wonder is emphasised again and again in the Śaiva *śāstras*. The ***Kulayukti***, in a cryptic definition of reflexive consciousness, which is the hall mark of Kāśmīr Śaivism says: "the discovery and the vision of the self through the self is a cause of wonder indeed."[139]

The Indian tradition lays great store in the act of seeing and higher knowledge or vision is called *darśana*, for *darśana* is not mere outward sight but inner vision. Repeatedly the Śaiva scriptures equate knowledge with seeing; for the *āgamas,* the act of seeing is the mode of knowledge *par excellence*. Śiva's self-discovery comes through a visual enjoyment, and therefore understanding, of Pārvatī and especially through the interaction of the *darpaṇa* of Pārvatī. Even the simple act of looking at oneself in a mirror produces child-like wonder in anyone, how much more amazement would there be at the self-discovery that the *darpaṇa* of Pārvatī causes in Śiva? There is here a clear and unambiguous affirmation of not only the need but the delight of objectivity in the process of self-knowledge, in complete and clear contradistinction to the nihilism of Śaṅkara's Advaita Vedānta and Buddhism. Objectivity no longer remains a hindrance but a doorway to self-discovery, not the source of *avidyā* but a stepping stone to *śuddha-vidyā*, not something that has to be rejected as an illusion but something that has to be joyously affirmed and celebrated, not an object of *karma* but of *kriyā*. To the ordinary person, wonderment comes from an encounter with something unusual and extraordinary but not so for the *sādhaka* who finds the expansion of his limited consciousness from his perception of ordinary objects as a source of wonder and delight. The integral activity of consciousness, free of all limitations, leads to bliss. For the Kāśmīr Śaivites, the experience of *spanda* is a source of wonder. This expansion of consciousness, the movement from *aham* to *aham idam* and then to *aham eva sarvam*, the growth from the limited *aham* to the expansive *viśvarūpam* is an aesthetic experience of wonder, an *adbhuta-rasa*, more enjoyable than other forms of meditation, such as that on *cakras* such as the *mulādhāra* or *bindu*.[140] It is the *darpaṇa* of Pārvatī that has converted an act of ordinary perception into an aesthetic experience leading Śiva into a state of creative contemplation or *bhāvanā*. Abhinavagupta defines *bhāvanā* as "that contemplation by which a thing though real and existent appeared as non-existent and unreal previously owing to obscurity and reappears as manifest reality by sheer clarity."[141] And it is in that act of *bhāvanā* that the cognising subject and the cognisable object have come together, joyously affirmed and held in dynamic harmony, a state of *śiva-śakti-sāmarasya*, a state represented by the joyous marriage of Śiva and Pārvatī and shown visually by the beautiful image of *ardhanārīśvara*. This act of perception of Pārvatī by Śiva becomes none other than an act of chanting a *mantra*, a *mantroccāra*. As Dyczkowski rightly says:

> "the term *uccāra* conveys different meanings according to the yogī's level of practise. At the individual level it is the recitation of *mantra* in harmony with the movement of the breath. At its height, it is the upward moving current of vitality through *suṣumnā*. At the empowered level, it is the persistent force of awareness that impels individual consciousness and merges it with universal consciousness."[142]

It is interesting to note that the *āgamas* use the analogy of the mirror when it refers to Śiva's universalised consciousness whereas in this essay we have emphasised the mirror in the hand of Pārvatī. For the *āgamācāryas* Śiva's universalised consciousness, vast and unfettered by the limited *aham*, contains the entire world, as a mirror contains the whole city, as a pure crystal takes up the appearance of the different hues reflected in it,[143] as the seed of the *nyagrodha* holds the entire tree and the juices of the egg of the peacock potentially contains the colours of the plumes.[144] To the free, unfettered and universalised Śiva all objective phenomena, outer or inner, are like his own body.[145] The mirror of Śiva, as opposed to the mirror of Pārvatī, is a statement of *bhairavatā* which has been defined as "resting in one's essential self"[146] and thus becomes a symbol of *viśrānti*. *Pārvatīdarpaṇa* on the other hand is the paradigm of *pratyabhijñā*, of cognition through recognition, which is the foundational principle of Kāśmīr Śaivism epistemology. It need hardly be emphasised that *pratyabhijñā* is an integral part of *viśrānti* and that therefore the *darpaṇa* of Pārvatī is an integral part of the *darpaṇa* of Śiva. It is the *Pārvatīdarpaṇa* that leads to *pratyabhijñā* and thereby creates the sense of wonder in Śiva and it is the mirror of Śiva that leads to *viśrānti*. Thus there are two mirrors facing each other. Through the all important step of *pratybhijñā*, *Pārvatīdarpaṇa* has not only united subject and object in the epistemic encounter but brought the realisation in that joyous and pulsating state of oneness that the "separation between subject and object is the product of a creative act and not of an illusion."[147] If art be the objectification of an idea and aesthetics the realisation of that idea through the art object, *Pārvatīdarpaṇa* is the epitomy of the perfect art object and *Śivadarpaṇa* the resting point of the subject in the epistemology of Kāśmīr Śaivism. In affirming the art object, and making it not only instrumental but inherent in Śiva's self-awareness, it is but fitting that this essay be called *Pārvatīdarpaṇa*. For unlike the *vedāntins*, the objective world and art objects in particular, for Kāśmīr Śaivites is not to be regarded as *māyā* and dismissed as an illusion, but is to be regarded as an object that has resulted from Śiva's *bhāvanā* or creative contemplation, and one that has to be deeply and meaningfully recognised and cognised.

The freedom and the ability of the absolute to appear in diverse forms is the Kāśmīr Śaivite understanding of *māyā*. Spontaneous and joyous differentiation rather than illusion or ignorance is the way in which *māyā* is understood in this system of philosophy. Śiva as the consummate subject, the *prabuddha*, ever alert, observes the *spanda* energy in all states, making a simple act of cognition an act of creative contemplation or *bhāvanā*, leading him not only into a state of heightened awareness but self-awareness.[148] It is that creative contemplation or *bhāvanā* that leads to spiritual satisfaction,[149] and it is *bhāvanā* that is to be regarded as *japa*.[150] The act of creative contemplation as envisaged by *bhāvanā* includes *dhāraṇā* (concentration), *dhyāna* (meditation) and *samādhi* (absorption).[151] Abhinavagupta states that the act of *bhāvanā*, if combined with practices such as *mantra, nyāsa* and *homa* leads to spiritual power.[152]

Chapter 6

Viśrānti

It has rightly been said that "the myths of Śiva have many levels. They have to be entered all at the same time, or else the total, multiple perspective of each is lost sight of."[153] The joyous wedding and the celebrations thereafter, take a different turn as Śiva turns away from his erotic persona to his ascetic. Some ominous signs, ominous however only to those who cannot comprehend the totality of Śiva's persona, had appeared even during the wedding ceremony, when Viṣṇu had lusted for Pārvatī, at which time Śiva had forewarned that his romantic involvement with Pārvatī was subject to interruptions. Even after the wedding Śiva had threatened to abandon Pārvatī if she did not trust him. And periodically, after the marriage, Śiva could not hide his true nature and would give into periods of isolation and quietudes, austerity and penance, much to the disapproval of Pārvatī's mother Menā. It is this other aspect of Śiva's persona that we need to understand, and for this we need to dip into the *purāṇas* and not merely *mahākāvyas*. For a *mahākāvya* merely dwells on Śiva's romantic nature, as does ***Kumārasaṁbhava***, for that is the mandate of a *kāvya*. A *kāvya*, therefore, can provide only a partial understanding of Śiva's nature. We must part company with *kavis* such as Kālidāsa and turn to *āgamācāryas* for that understanding. It is worth repeating that for Kāśmīr Śaivites, Śiva is just another name for consciousness, now Śiva's, now ours. For Utpaladeva clearly states that although appearing in many forms Śiva is the essence of consciousness.[154] And then again in the words of Utpaladeva "in this unconscious world you (Śiva) are the form of consciousness."[155]

It would be very easy to dismiss the asceticism of Śiva as an aberration or contradiction, as has been done by some mythologists, for on the surface, it is indeed such a contrast to his romantic and erotic aspect. The romantic and the erotic are easy to celebrate, but the ascetic and the quiescent need a thoughtful understanding. As long as we view Śiva as a mythic person we are likely to remain in a trap and view Śiva's asceticism as something that does not befit a romantic. However it should not take long for a Kāśmīr Śaivite to realise that the mythic Śiva is just an anthropomorphic symbol of the vast and unbounded consciousness, the very same *satyam bṛhat* or the consciousness that Vedic poets eulogised. The concept of retreat into subjectivity, which is the essence of *viśrānti*, does not quite fit in when one is engaged in enjoying the ***Śiva Purāṇa*** as pure narrative, which emphasises his romance and marriage to Pārvatī. However, when one undertakes an enjoyment of the narrative as a paradigm for epistemology, it becomes clear that Śiva's asceticism is as much a part of him as is his eroticism, his periods of quietude as integral a part of him as his romantic activity, his aloofness from Pārvatī as important as his *āliṅgana* of her, the *śānta-rasa* as much a part of Śiva as *śṛṅgāra-rasa*, for it is only through the alternating phases of the *rasas* that the throbbing reality of Śiva can be realised. One phase would not be complete without the other, actually one phase complements the other, and to state even further one phase activates the other just as the indrawing breath leads to the outgoing breath; this is the defining feature of *spanda*, which is the essence of Śiva and therefore of consciousness itself. It is obvious that two throbs of *spanda*, like two breaths, must be interspersed with a period of rest and quietudes.

Pārvatī and her parents were suitably forewarned of this aspect of Śiva's personality in the narrative in many different ways and if they did not pick up on the hint it was because they were engrossed in the emotional events of the marriage. Concerned as they were with their daughter's material happiness they were pleased as long as Śiva was romantic and attentive. Throughout the narrative there are instances where Śiva's other side is made known to us. We are given glimpses and subtle hints that Śiva indeed has another side. At one point seven *ṛṣis* were deputed by Śiva to test Pārvatī's resolve. They approached Pārvatī and tried to dissuade her from undertaking austerities to win Śiva. They described Śiva thus:

> O young lady, He for whose sake, you are performing this elaborate penance is a perpetually indifferent person, without any emotion. Undoubtedly he is an enemy of Kāma.
>
> The trident bearing Śiva has an inauspicious body, devoid of shame and has no home or pedigree. He is naked and ill-featured. He associates with ghosts and goblins and the like.
>
> A befitting bridegroom for you is lord Viṣṇu endowed with all good qualities. He is a resident of Vaikuṇṭha, lord of wealth and is skilled in sports.[156]
>
> O Pārvatī, with him we shall fix your marriage that will confer happiness on you. Leave off this obstinacy. Be happy.[157]

However Pārvatī was firm in her resolve and this is what she told the sages:

> O excellent sages, what you have said may be true according to your light and wisdom; but O brahmins, my tenacity cannot be affected.
>
> Śiva is Brahman, unchanging and without aberration. He assumes shapes and forms for the welfare of his devotees. He does not make a show of worldly lordship.
>
> Interest in embellishments and ornaments shall be found in those who are deluded by illusion and who are not in unison with Brahman. The lord is devoid of attributes, unborn, free from illusion, of invisible movement and a cosmic being.
>
> Even if the sun were to rise in the west, even if the mountain Meru were to move, even if fire were to be cool and even if the lotus were to bloom on a rock at the top of a mountain, my resolve cannot change. This is the truth.[158]

When the *ṛṣis* reported back to the Mountain King and recommended to Parvata that he give his daughter in marriage to Śiva, Menā "however was less certain about the wisdom of giving her daughter in marriage to Śiva, whose only qualification, if it were one, was his asceticism."[159] Pārvatī was tested and given a foretaste of Śiva's true nature, albeit in a cryptic form, yet another time, when Śiva took on the disguise of an old and decrepit beggar and expressed his surprise at so beautiful a girl intent on marrying a mad and wandering ascetic. This is how the beggar described Śiva to Pārvatī:

> The great lord is bull bannered. His body is smeared with ashes. His hair is matted. He is clad in the hide of a tiger. He has covered his body with the hide of an elephant.
>
> He holds the skull. Serpents twine round his limbs. Poison has left a mark on his neck. He eats even forbidden food. He has odd eyes and is definitely awful.
>
> You are a jewel among women. Your father is the king of all mountains. Why do you crave for a husband like this and that too by means of severe penance?
>
> Handing over a gold coin you wish to buy a piece of glass. Setting aside the pure sandal paste you wish to smear mud over your body.[160]

Pārvatī once again expresses her firm resolve to marry Śiva. And this is what she says to the decrepit beggar:

> I know the real form of Śiva.
>
> He is in fact devoid of attributes. But for some reason he takes up attributes. How can he have a birth, he who is really attributeless but takes up attributes?
>
> Sadāśiva is the support and receptacle of all lores. Of what avail is learning to him who is perfect and the supreme soul?[161]

The final portend of Śiva's asceticism comes during the wedding ceremony itself. As the invited guests wait expectantly, Himavat invites Śiva to participate in the *gotroccāra* and identify his pedigree and lineage. He says:

> O Śiva! please do not delay. Please mention your genealogy, saintly lineage, family name and your Veda along with your branch of the Veda.[162]

At this point Nārada spoke thus:

> O mountain! even Viṣṇu, Brahmā and other gods do not know his *gotra*, family and name. What then can be said about others?

> It was a result of the severe penance of Pārvatī that Śiva was seen by you. O mountain! in one day according to whose calculation a crore of Brahmā's become annihilated.
>
> He is the formless supreme *brahman*. He is attributeless. He is greater than primordial nature. He has no shape, is free from aberrations. He is the master of delusion. He is greater than the greatest.
>
> He has no *gotra*, family or name. He is independent. He is favourably disposed to his devotees. At his will he assumes many bodies taking many names. He is full of attributes.
>
> He is *sugotrin* as well devoid of *gotra*. He is of noble family as well as devoid of a family. Thanks to Pārvatī's penance he has now become your son-in-law. There is no doubt about it.
>
> The whole world consisting of the mobile and the immobile has been deluded by him in His divine sport. O excellent mountain even the wisest of men does not know Him.[163]

Indications and hints of the ascetic aspect of Śiva were given and should have been realised by the spiritually adept and alert. A clear distinction is seen in the character of Menā and Pārvatī. While Menā swoons and demonstrates other acts of hysteria at Śiva's ascetic nature, Pārvatī, being spiritually adept, on the other hand recognises that asceticism is an integral part of Śiva's romanticism, for while she is a participant in the narrative, she is after all a *yoginī* in own right. For she clearly says:

> The form of Śiva, the supreme soul is that of *Brahman*, devoid of attributes. How can people like you know it, people with extrovert faces (and hedonistic tendencies)?[164]

It is this misunderstood aspect of Śiva that needs to be explained, not through social or psychological interpretations but through the epistemology of Kāśmīr Śaivism, which affords a beautiful interpretation and understanding of Śiva's persona.

The romantic aspect of Śiva corresponds to the *savikalpa* cognition that Śiva undertakes, the dynamics of which were discussed in the preceding section. This included the progression from "*aham*" to "*aham idam*" and finally to "*aham eva sarvam*". The importance of the *darpaṇa* of Pārvatī, the emotion of wonder, the *sāmarasya* of Śiva and Pārvatī and the image of the *ardhanārīśvara* were all emphasised in that dynamics. Having availed of the *sākṣātartha* and soaked his mind with sensory information arising from Pārvatī, it is time for Śiva to move inwards and seek the *parokṣārtha* of the encounter with Pārvatī, it is time for the subject after its encounter with the object to assert its subjectivity, it is time not only for the mind but the "*manaso manaḥ*" or the mind of the mind, it is time to realise the true nature of the self. The Upaniṣads constantly remind us that "it is the ear of the ear, the mind of the mind, the tongue of the tongue, the breath of the breath and the eye of the eye" that really cognises.[165] The two stages of knowledge, an initial *savikalpa* and the ultimate *nirvikalpa jñāna*, is a constant refrain of the Upaniṣads. The ***Kaṭha Upaniṣad*** points to the all important concept of epistemic rest when it says:

> "When all the senses are stilled, when the mind is at rest, when the intellect wavers not, then say the wise, is reached the highest state.
>
> This calm of the senses and the mind has been defined as *yoga*. He who attains it is freed from delusion."[166]

The strongly Idealistic stance of the Upaniṣads and its affirmation of *nirvikalpa jñāna*, or non-cognitive awareness, as the highest reality runs like a thread throughout. The dialogue between the master and the student in the ***Chāndogya Upaniṣad*** that ends with the affirmation by the master "verily my dear that finest essence which you do not perceive—verily, my dear from that finest essence this great *Nyagrodha* tree thus arises,"[167] establishes the supremacy of *nirvikalpa jñāna*. The ***Śvetāśvatara Upaniṣad*** which talks of the two birds of the self-same feathers, one of which eats sweet fruit and is deluded and the other which just watches and is serene, is not only a reference to the two types of cognitions, but characterises *nirvikalpa jñāna* as serene, supreme and established in subjectivity. While upholding the supremacy of *nirvikalpa jñāna,* the Upaniṣads do not address the question of the status of *savikalpa jñāna*. It is this serenity of *nirvikalpa jñāna* that the Kāśmīr Śaivites capture in their concept of *viśrānti* and which in turn is beautifully demonstrated by periods of isolation and quietudes of Śiva in the narrative. The ***Mālinīvijayavārtika*** says:

> Just as every drop of water comes to rest in the ocean, so all acts and cognitions (come to rest) in the Great Lord, the ocean of consciousness. Even a little water on the ground drunk by the sun's rays goes as rain to the great ocean. Similarly all knowledge and action in the universe merge in the ocean of Śiva either spontaneously and evidently by itself or (indirectly) through a series of other (processes).[168]

While the process of self-awareness needs cognitive activity, perfect self-awareness leads to stillness or *viśrānti.* This is the culmination of awareness when it rests in itself alone, in its primordial self, enjoying the pure awareness of 'I', the *ahaṁ-vimarśa.* When awareness rests in itself and contemplates its own nature, it sees itself as the pure subject that unfolds as the unity of all things."[169] The all important concept of *viśrānti* of Kāśmīr Śaivism is a rich and full epistemic rest, it is the rest that comes at the culmination of joyful activity, it is the pleasurable stillness that succeeds the excitement of orgasm, it is the silence that follows speech and yet contains within it all sounds, it is the glow of restful knowledge that seeks knowledge no more, it is the serenity of self-awareness that need not look outward anymore, but only inward to enjoy that awareness, it is the stillness of self-reflection, it is the freedom of consciousness turning in on itself, it is the beauty of a cosmic vision, it is the glory and majesty of *viśvarūpa.*[170] This *viśrānti* is not the contentless *nirvikalpa jñāna* of Śaṅkara or the *śūnyatā* of Nāgārjuna but a rich and primal subjectivity driven by its objectivity reflecting on itself. As Abhinavagupta has said, "that which is conscious necessarily reflects on itself."[171] The ***Śiva Sūtras*** has declared "by constant awareness of the pure principle he becomes like one in whom the binding power existing in the limited self is absent."[172] Having enjoyed *śiva-śakti-sāmarasya*, the bliss of oneness with Pārvatī, as seen in the romantic bliss of Śiva and Pārvatī in the narrative or the dynamic harmony of the *ardhanārīśvara* in the plastic arts, the epistemic drive towards perfection makes this bliss itself a source of bondage,[173] and Śiva seeks a state of freedom even beyond it, namely towards *paramaśiva. Paramaśiva*, is Śiva's primal self, of pure unbound consciousness, of pristine subjectivity, of repose unsullied even by bliss, *nirānanda*, of still awareness undisturbed by thought constructs, a state of *nirvikalpa*.[174] This is the experience of *viśrānti* as portrayed by Śiva's solitariness, aloofness and asceticism in the narrative, and equally beautifully illustrated by depictions of Śiva shown in solitude in a cave in Kailāsa in the various miniature paintings. In the state of *viśrānti* the objective world is not excluded, as is in Śaṅkara's *nirguṇa brahman*, but "the entire world is (included) simultaneously (but) without thought-constructs as a form of higher consciousness."[175] It is only in that state of *viśrānti*, the joyous and quiet state of *viśvarūpa*, of the stillness that has followed the romantic affirmation and indulgence of the world, that Śiva can unwaveringly assert that "I am Śiva, the essence of the universe."[176] Prior to this Śiva's consciousness was limited and the state of knowledge could be captured by the words "*aham idam*". It is only in the state of *viśrānti*, that consciousness has been fully universalised and he declares, "*viśvarūpo aham idam*".

It is important to distinguish the *viśrānti* of Kāśmīr Śaivism from the passive and dormant *nirguṇa brahman* of Śaṅkara's Advaita Vedānta, for the two are incorrectly taken as similar. In Śaṅkara's Advaita Vedānta the *nirguṇa* state is arrived at by negating the *saguṇa* as *mithyā* or illusion, whereas the Kāśmīr Śaivites emphasise that "*śakti* assumes the shape of a *bindu* which helps it return to Śiva and rest."[177] Herein, in the concept of *bindu*, lies the fundamental difference between the limited *advaita* of Śaṅkara and the rich and affirmative *advaita* of Kāśmīr Śaivism, between *vidyā* of Śaṅkara and *sadvidyā* of Abhinavagupta. While, for Śaṅkara, *savikalpa jñāna* is a hindrance which must be overcome, for indulgence in it is ignorance or *avidyā*, for the Kāśmīr Śaivites on the other hand, *śakti* or *savikalpa jñāna* in the form of *bindu*, is the door to the realisation of *nirvikalpa jñāna*. *Savikalpa jñāna* cannot be bypassed or ignored for the assertion and affirmation of this stage of cognition not only leads to *nirvikalpa jñāna*, but that initial *savikapla jñāna* born out of cognition of objects and its joyous affirmation, persists in the subject. We have Abhinavagupta's assurance on this point when he says that "all objects shine within that subject".[178] For the Kāśmīr Śaivites the "resting of both the I-consciousness or *aham*, and the this-consciousness or *idam*, on one substratum is called *sadvidyā*."[179]

The significance of the *bindu* is central to the epistemology of Kāśmīr Śaivism and in particular in the proper understanding of its concept of *viśrānti*. For it explains how the object itself drives the subject into that state of cognitive serenity and rest. Perfect cognition, as does perfect utterance of a *mantra*, ends in a *bindu*, and it is the *bindu* which drives that cognition and utterance to a state of rest.

To understand this concept of *bindu* it is essential to probe the mystery of *mātṛkā* or *mantra-śakti*, a branch of study equally dear to Kāśmīr Śaivites. The *bindu* is compared to the *anusvāra*, the dot on the letter "*h*" which produces the sound "*m*" in the word *aham* and drives the vibrating and pulsating utterance of *aham* into a serene silence. In the various *maṇḍalas,* the *bindu* occupies the pride of place and is centrally located within the cosmic triangles. In the *ānanda-tāṇḍava* of the dancing Naṭarāja it is this *bindu* that is represented by the left earring of Śiva. In no state of Śiva is Pārvatī excluded, no state of *ānanda* is complete without the *bindu*. This is the strength and the cardinal feature of Kāśmīr Śaivism. The *savikalpa* stage of *jñāna* is the stage of enthusiastic, romantic and assiduous inquiry, where the cognising mind indulges in the object, creating *vidyā* and leading the mind to creative contemplation or *bhāvanā*. In this stage Pārvatī as an object of cognition appears in all her splendour and glory, an object to be cognitively indulged, celebrated and enjoyed. However after a full and complete cognition, as after the enunciation of the cosmic sounds "*a*" and "*h*", it is the *bindu* that must bring activity to a period of rest, it must lead the mind from *vidyā* to *sadvidyā*, only so that the next pulsation of activity can start all over again. Without the restful vibration of the *bindu*, speech as well as cognition would be driven to a stage of hedonism and to a point of exhaustion. It is the *bindu* that brings about the gap, the interval, between two breaths, as between two *cittavṛttis*. This *bindu* is not a mere passive process but an active force. Kṣemarāja says:

> O dear one, just as a bird of prey glimpsing in the sky a piece

> of meat (flung to it) quickly catches it with the speed natural to it, so should the best of *yogīs* catch hold of the light of consciousness (*manobindu*). Just as an arrow fixed to a bow and drawn with great force flies forth, so beloved, does *bindu* fly forward with the force of awareness (*uccāreṇa*).[180]

The *bindu* brings the utterance and the cognition to a restful conclusion, *sadvidyā* or *viśrānti*, and leads the mind to the bliss, the calm and the catholic vastness, and the universality of the knowledge of pure subjectivity. This state of knowledge is the *vidyā-śarīra-sattā* that the *śāstra* talks about and which is further characterised as *aśeṣa-viśvabhedamaya-pūrṇāhaṁ-vimarśa-sphurattā* or the luminous being of the perfect I-consciousness which is non-different from the entire cosmos. This indeed is the secret of the *mantra*.[181] The Upaniṣads have dwelt at length on the dynamics of the cosmic sound *Oṁ*. The mantra *aham* is to Kāśmīr Śaivites what *Oṁ* is to the Upaniṣads. The ***Muṇḍaka Upaniṣad*** has said,

> "The mystic syllable *Oṁ* is the bow. The arrow is the soul. *Brahman* is said to be the mark. By the undestructed man is to be penetrated.[182]

The concept of *viśrānti* not only points to the primacy of the primal self or the subject as the driving and sustaining force of the epistemic encounter but equally highlights the permanence of the self or 'I'-consciousness, an idea that is shared by all Idealistic systems and in particular by Kāśmīr Śaivism, Śaṅkara's Advaita Vedānta and Rāmānuja's Viśiṣṭādvaita. The ***Spandakārikā*** states quite clearly that even though there are different states such as *jāgrata, svapna* and *suṣupta* or waking, dreaming and deep sleep, at the mundane level and states such as *dhāraṇā, dhyāna* and *samādhi*, or concentration, meditation and intense absorption, at the level of the *yogī*, it is the *spanda* principle that remains as the uninterrupted, unbroken, ground of all states.[183] The ***Spandakārikā*** is quite unequivocal when it states that while manifestation of consciousness may differ as do waking from the dream states, the underlying consciousness is unchanged. Consciousness is not transformed, for transformation can only occur in the insentient and the process of transformation can never apply to the sentient.[184] Śiva retreats into isolation and solitude, after his romantic involvement with Pārvatī, to not only emphasise and realise pure subjectivity but reflect upon that self-same subjectivity that sustained and supported his amorous togetherness with Pārvatī. Śiva's *viśrānti* is not in any sense a transformation. For Kāśmīr Śaivites it is Śiva himself that is the ever-present experient or subject in all states.[185] The keyword for Kāśmīr Śaivites in considering different states of consciousness is *tadabhinne* or "not different from that" and in taking this position they assert that while the objective content of a particular situation will vary, the underlying subject is constant and never changing. Kāśmīr Śaivites in no uncertain terms reject the concept of *pariṇāma* or transformation advocated by Sāṁkhya and equally the concept of *vivartta* or illusion advocated by Śaṅkara's Advaita Vedānta. Thus the different phases of Śiva-Pārvatī-vivāha starting with Śiva courting Pārvatī, and then Śiva riding the Nandī on his way to Oṣadhiprastha followed by Śiva's joyously romantic association with her in Kailāsa and then finally Śiva in a state of ascetic solitude are only different manifestations of Śiva held together by the same primal and subjective experient. This is particularly and strikingly brought out by the *darpaṇa* of Pārvatī in the androgyn image of *ardhanārīśvara* in which the mirror reflects back to Śiva his own image, emphasising that once an object is firmly and rigorously affirmed and enjoyed, it reveals through that objective experience none other than the experiencing self. The lordship of the subject in the epistemic process is also brought home visually in the tender togetherness of Śiva and Pārvatī in which Pārvatī is depicted either serving Śiva or even serving Śiva's snake. The object while maintaining its bonafides is ultimately subservient to the subject. During the entire process there has not been a transformation of consciousness, neither has there been an objective illusion. The romantic and the ascetic are two aspects of Śiva, different in the objective content and yet the same in its subjective underpinning. Utpala Bhaṭṭa sums up the same idea in the following verse:

> The difference is of the states and not of the experient who holds them; just as there is a difference in the various parts of the lotus but not in the basic property (*śakti*) of the lotus.[186]

It is a cardinal feature of Kāśmīr Śaivism that posits the subject, the primordial Śiva, as the common binding reality, *anusandhātā*, of the different states. This is the strength and the freedom, *svātantrya*, of Śiva. Abhinavagupta affirms this in no uncertain terms when he says:

> Thus action which is nothing more than the free consciousness, manifesting itself both internally and externally, in accordance with the temporal order; therefore action really belongs to the subject. Hence the powers of action and knowledge are mutually inseparable.[187]

And it is that primordial and transcendent Śiva that contains the whole world from "*sadāśiva* down to the earth".[188] And since the whole world is nothing other than Śiva, the *āgamācāryas*, "make the objective world an object of knowledge in order to reveal the primordial self."[189] The different states of consciousness born of the "indivisible powers of knowledge and action"[190] are merely *ābhāsas* or reflections of the underlying, transcendent Śiva. The biune unity of knowledge and action, is the defining feature of Kāśmīr Śaivism, and is stressed again and again.[191] It is the manifestation of knowledge and action through space and time that leads to various reflections.[192] Śaṅkara's *brahman* on the other hand is passive and devoid of activity and not much can be said of it. The solitary Śiva, apparently turning away from romanticising with Pārvatī in the narrative, represents this primordial, transcendent subject, ever causing different manifestations like reflections, but never ceasing to be the ground of all those manifestations. It is important to point out that Kālidāsa chooses not to carry the narrative beyond the romantic phase of Śiva-Pārvatī-vivāha, for Kālidāsa, unlike Abhinavagupta is a poet and a storyteller and not an *āgamācarya*. But students of the *āgamas* that we are, we cannot let our epistemic adventure rest when the curtain falls on the drama of Śiva and Pārvatī, but we must, continue our explorations beyond the dramatic termination "they lived happily ever after". For unless we do that we become mere superficial spectators at a drama unable to continue the epistemic hints and suggestions that we received during the narrative. By the same token we cannot ignore the fact that in the visually arresting image of the *ardhanārīśvara*, Śiva is anatomically larger than Pārvatī, indicating that the subject drives the epistemic encounter and it is in the subject that the experience rests finally and it behooves us to investigate fully that subject and not stop at the object. For it is in that state of epistemic rest that the "objective world shines in the luminous mirror of the self"[193] and it is through that epistemic rest that the subject "retains his essential nature intact."[194] As aestheticians we must not be satisfied with *sākṣātārtha* but proceed to investigate the richer and fuller *parokṣārtha*, and thereby convert the art experience into a knowledge episode, and bring epistemic activity to a period of epistemic rest. As the *āgamas* have said,[195] this epistemic rest, this end point of our exploration, this termination of the adventure of knowledge, this homeward journey of the traveller, this culmination of the aesthetic experience is the restful, subjective self, none other than Śiva, where the *aham* and the *idam*, the subject and the object become one. And of this subjective, restful Śiva it has been said that there can "never be disappearance of that inner nature which is the abode of omniscience." [196] For in that *antarmukho bhāvaḥ, jñāna* and *kriyā*, rest as does the banyan tree in the seed.[197] These and other statements from the *āgamas* are enough to assure us that the restful Śiva is not *śūnya* or void in the Mādhaymika sense, neither passive in the *vedāntic* sense, but dynamic as *spanda* itself, throbbing with life, richly radiant, realising that "it is I, the highest self."[198] That epistemic rest, the *viśrānti* of Kāśmīr Śaivism, is a state of realisation, a state of bliss born of knowledge, but not in itself an object of knowledge and therefore not subject to the modes of cognition.[199] To make *viśrānti* an object of knowledge would create infinite regress, requiring one knowledge to certify another. The certitude of *viśrānti* is in the realisation in that restful state, that the whole world, given to us through the mode of *pratyakṣa* or perception, is a play of Śiva,[200] and that if we are to adore that Śiva we must become Śiva ourselves.

Chapter 7

Epilogue

Salutations to Śiva, the dweller of Kailāsa and lord of Umā, who teaches the richness of *advaita* through his amorous relationship with Pārvatī. 1.

Hail to Śaṅkara, consort of Gaurī, whose head holds the Gaṅgā
The bearer of the *triśūla*, the insignia of *jñāna, kriyā* and *icchā*. 2.

For the chariot of *citta* is driven by *icchā*
and its riders are *jñāna* and *kriyā*. 3.

It has been said that self-awareness comes from activity
but perfect self-awareness leads to stillness. 4.

For to know is to create duality
but to realise is to enjoy oneness
A oneness that embraces duality and yet feels a oneness. 5.

The great Maheśa, searching within himself
in his quest for knowledge
Dispassionate, oblivious of himself and the world around
is aroused by Pārvatī, she of perfect beauty
Herself a *yoginī* and destined to be Śiva's *vāma*. 6.

There ensues a dialogue, between the dweller of Kailāsa
and the daughter of the mountain
Pārvatī espousing Sāṁkhya the embodiment of *savikalpa jñāna* and

Śiva speaking Vedānta which is the essence of *nirvikalpa jñāna*. 7.

For have not the Upaniṣads spoken of two birds
of the self-same feathers?
one busy, the other still
one eating sweet fruit, the other sitting still
for sweet indeed is *savikalpa*, but sweeter still
the stillness of *nirvikalpa*. 8.

A spirited, dialogue, a tussle of words, a throb in the *citta*
Between Śiva, the eternal subject, the perfect *aham*
And Pārvatī, the consummate object, the sensuous *idam*
One wanting to embrace the other but afraid of losing oneself
A mighty enigma indeed. 9.

For both cherish the majesty and grandeur of *advaita* where oneness reigns and unity prevails
But yet beautiful indeed is *dvaita*, self-respectful and mindful of its unique existence. 10.

The dialogue must heal the *viraha*, the dalliance must lead to a solution of the epistemic riddle
As the devoted Nandī stands in vigil and even Brahmā awaits the outcome of the encounter of Śiva and Pārvatī. 11.

Śiva's first cognition discovers the sensuous Pārvatī, but he cognises yet again and sees the mirror in her hand.
The first cognition reveals, the lustful Pārvatī, the second cognition none other than Śiva himself
in the mirror of Pārvatī. 12.

Śiva is wonderstruck, he experiences the *rasa* of *adbhuta*
at the transformation brought about by the mirror
a movement from the enigmatic *dvaita* to restful *advaita*
such is the wonder of *pratyabhijñā* that creates the majestic *advaita* not the *advaita* of negation but of affirmation, not where the mind whispers *neti-neti*
but where the *citta* joyously exclaims *iti iti*. 13.

The devotees rejoice, Nandī is radiant and Brahmā is pleased
Himavat and Menā receive the guests and the marriage fire is lit, and *mantras* are chanted
Viṣṇu is the honoured guest and Lakṣmī leads the bride
The residents of Oṣadhiprastha partake of the celebrations. 14

Śiva's tender *āliṅgana* amorously holds Pārvatī, just as *śabda* embraces *artha*
The divine couple perform the dance of *ardhanārīśvara*
and the *brahmajijñāsu* learns the lessons of *advaita*. 15.

Endnotes

1. *tanyate vistāryate jñānam anena iti tantram.* This etymology of Tantra is given by Bhattacharya in ***History of the Tantric Religion.***
2. ***History of the Tantric Religion.*** Bhattacharya. p. 3.
3. *kṛte śrutyukta ācārastretāyāṁ smṛti-saṁbhavaḥ. dvāpare tu purāṇoktaḥ, kalāvāgamasaṁmataḥ.*
   Kulārṇava Tantra, quoted in ***Śakti and Śākta.*** p. 7.
4. Pupul Jaykar, *The Times of India*, Sunday Review, March 27, 1983, p.II.
5. ***Another Harmony.*** p. 17.
6. *vitarka vicāra ānanda asmitā rūpānugamāt samprajñātaḥ.*
   Yogasūtra. 1.17
7. *yatra yatra manastuṣṭir, manas tatraiva dhārayet.*
   Vijñānabhairava. 74.
8. ***History of the Tantric Religion.*** p. 10.
9. *jñānam vimarśānuprāṇitam*
   Īśvara Pratyabhijñā Vimarśinī. II. p. 215.
10. *āgamastu īśvarasya antaraṅga eva vyāpāraḥ.*
    Īśvara Pratyabhijñā Vimarśinī. II. p. 84.
11. *iti tad anusāreṇa padārtha-nirṇayaṁ viśvaprameyīkaraṇapratilabdha-tadviśvottīrṇa-pramātṛpada-hṛdayaṅgamīkārābhiprāyeṇa.*
    Īśvara Pratyabhijñā Vimarśinī. II. p. 213.
12. ***Viśvasāra Tantra,*** quoted in ***Śakti and Śākta.*** p. 37.
13. ***Śakti and Śākta.*** p. 37.
14. ***ibid.*** p. 51.
15. ***ibid.*** p. 29.
16. ***Tantra, The Indian Cult of Ecstasy***. p. 9.
17. ***ibid.*** p. 14.
18. *parivṛtya ānandarūpaṁ hṛdayasvabhāvaparasaṁvidātmaka-śivavimarśa-tādātmyam.*
    Parātrīśikā Vivaraṇa. p. 11 (text).
19. ***Parātrīśikā Vivaraṇa*** p. 35.
20. *idantātmakaṁ viśvābhāsaṁ ahantātmani pūrṇābhāse saṁsthānam.*
    quoted by Jaideva Singh in ***Parātrīśikā Vivarana.*** p. 35, note 7.

21. *tattvataḥ kasyacin naitad.*
Vijñānabhairava. 99.
22. *sarvatra bhairavo bhāvaḥ sāmānyeṣv api gocaraḥ.*
Vijñānabhairava. 124.
23. *na dveṣaṁ bhāvayet kvāpi na rāgam bhāvayet kvacit.*
Vijñānabhairava. 126.
24. *yatra yatra mano yāti bāhye vābhyantarepi vā/ tatra tatra śivāvasthā.*
Vijñānabhairava. 116.
25. *ciddharmā sarvadeheṣu viśeṣo nāsti kutracit.*
Vijñānabhairava. 100.
26. *bhāvayed bharitāvasthām mahānandas tato bhavet.*
Vijñānabhairava. 72.
27. **Vijñānabhairava.** 69, 70, 71, 72, 73.
28. *etad uktam bhavati aham eva tatsaṁvedana rūpeṇa tādātmyapratipattito viśvaśarīraś cidānandaghanaḥ śiva iti saṁkalpo.*
The Yoga of Vibration and Divine Pulsation. p. 122-123.
29. *śivo bhūtvā śivaṁ yajet.*
The Yoga of Vibration and Divine Pulsation. p. 122-123.
30. **The Mythic Image.** p. 44.
31. *padmapatraśata-vyatibheda-nayena.*
This original quotation by Abhinavagupta has in turn been quoted by all commentators including Mammaṭa and Viśvanātha.
see ***Kāvyaprakāśa.*** Vol. 1. p. 62.
32. **The Sacred Marriage of a Hindu Goddess.** Harman. p. 149.
33. **The Advaita of Art.**
In my book I have argued that *rasa* and *rūpa* outside the strict confines of religion are capable of providing a transcendent experience to a prepared aesthete.
34. **Vaiṣṇava Iconography in the Tamil Country.** p. 209.
35. The iconological description of *Pārvatī tapasvinī* is taken from **Tapasvinī Pārvatī.**
36. **The Sacred Marriage of a Hindu Goddess.** p. 150.
37. *ibid.* pp.147-148.
38. **The Hour of God and Other Writings.** p. 198.
39. **Abhinavagupta: An Historical and Philosophical Study.** p. 401.
40. *avidyākṛtam kāryaprapañcam.*
Śaṅkara's *bhāṣya* on the **Brahma Sūtra**, 1.3.1.
quoted by Radhakrishnan in **Indian Philosophy.** p. 579.
41. *brahmaṇo hi vidyāikarūpasya katham avidyārūpatā.*
Īśvara Pratyabhijñā Vimarśinī. p. II. p. 202.
42. *na hi mṛgatṛṣṇikādayo'pi nirāspadā bhavanti.*
Śaṅkara's *bhāṣya* on the **Bhagavad-Gītā.** 13.14
quoted by Radhakrishnan in **Indian Philosophy.** p. 583.
43. *atra anirvacanīyavāde nā'nupattir dūṣaṇam.*
quoted by Radhakrishnan in **Indian Philosophy.** p. 578.

44. *nirvikalpo nirākārarūpo.*
Śaṅkara's ***Ātmaśataka.***
45. *dehendriya-mano-buddhi-prakṛtibhyo vilakṣaṇam.*
Ātmabodha. Śaṅkarācārya. verse 18.
46. *rogān iva rasāyanam.*
Ātmabodha. 37.
47. ***Indian Philosophy.*** p. 655.
48. ***The Development of Hindu Iconography.*** p. 553.
49. ***ibid.*** p. 115.
50. ***ibid.*** p. 475-476.
51. ***ibid.*** p. 233, p. 465, p. 476.
52. ***The Presence of Śiva.*** p. 456.
53. ***Nepal, Where the Gods are Young.*** p. 127.
54. O'Flaherty, Wendy Doniger, ***Women, Androgynes and Other Mythical Beasts.*** p. 290.
55. ***The History of Religions.*** Eliade, M. quoted by Muller-Ortega in ***The Triadic Heart of Śiva.*** p. 13.
56. Pupul Jaykar, ***The Times of India***, Sunday Review, March 23, 1983, p. II
57. *teṣām īśvarapratyabhijñā upadeśa-tattvaṁ manāk unmīlyate.*
Pratyabhijñāhṛdayam. p. 46.
58. ***Indian Idealism.*** Dasgupta. p. 27.
59. ***Tantrāloka*** 6.15
quoted by Dyczkowski in ***The Doctrine of Vibration.*** p.44.
60. *etad anaṅgikāräddhi māyāvedāntādinirṇītasyātmanaḥ svasphuraṇāmodamāndyalakṣaṇam asatkalpatvāpatitam* in ***Maheśrvarānanda's Mahārthamañjarī*** quoted by Jaideva Singh in ***Pratyabhijñāhṛdayam*** p. 23.
61. *śivo bhūtva yajeteti bhakto bhūtveti kathyate I*
tvameva hi vapuḥ sāraṁ bhaktair advyaśodhitam II
Śivastotrāvalī. 1.14
62. ***Īśvara Pratyabhijñā Vṛtti Vimarśinī.***
quoted in ***The Doctrine of Vibration.*** p. 92.
63. ***The Doctrine of Vibration.*** p. 92.
64. ***Chāndogyopaniṣad.*** 6.2.1-3.
quoted by Jaideva Singh in ***Pratyabhijñāhṛdayam.*** p. 9.
65. *jñānaṁ kriyā ca bhūtānāṁ jīvatāṁ jīvanaṁ matam I*
iti tathā ca jīvanam jñānakriye eva iti II
Paratrīśikā Vivaraṇa. p. 9 (text).
66. ***The Doctrine of Vibration.*** p. 43.
67. *citsāmānyaspandabhūḥ unmeṣātmā vyākhyātavyā.*
Pratyabhijñāhṛdayam. p. 113.
68. See note number 54.
69. *sa eva viśvameṣituṁ jñātuṁ kartuṁ conmukho bhavan I śaktisvabhāvaḥ kathito hṛdaya-trikoṇa-madhumāṁsalollāsaḥ II* ***Maheśvarānanda*** in

Mahārthamañjarī quoted by Jaideva Singh in ***Pratybhijñahṛdayam*** p. 9.

70. *grāhyagrāhakasaṁvittiḥ sāmānyā sarvadehinām I yogināṁ tu viśeṣoyam sambandhe sāvadhānatā II*
Pratyabhijñāhṛdayam. p. 50.
71. *pūrvapakṣatayā yena viśvam ābhāsya bhedataḥ I abhedottara-pakṣāntaṁ nīyate taṁ stumaḥ śivam II*
Īśvara Pratyabhijñā Vimarśinī. I. p. 81.
72. *namaste bhava-saṁbhrānta-bhrāntimudbhāvya bhindate I jñānānandaṁ ca nirdvandvaṁ deva vṛtvā vivṛṇvate II*
Īśvara Pratyabhijñā Vimarśinī. I. p. 82.
73. ***The Doctrine of Vibration.*** p. 24.
74. ***Parātrīśikā Vivaraṇa.*** p. 35.
75. *sakayosya jagat kṛtsnam śaktimāṁstu maheśvaraḥ.*
Parātrīśikā Vivaraṇa. p. 13 (text).
76. *svātmā sarvabhāvasvabhāvaḥ svayaṁ prakāśamānaḥ svātmānam eva svātmāvibhinnena praśnaprativacanena praṣṭṛprativaktṛ-svātmamayena ahantayā camatkurvan vimṛśatī.*
Parātrīśikā Vivaraṇa. p. 15.
77. *dhyānādi-bhāvaṁ smṛtireva labdhvā, cintāmaṇistvadvibhavaṁ vyanakti.*
Īśvara Pratyabhijñā Viamrśinī. I. p. 154.
78. *padārtharatnakiram nijahrdjapujitam, granthanantam smṛti sutrantaha santaiva stumaha śivam.*
Īśvara Pratyabhijñā Vimarsini. I. p. 147.
79. ***Śiva Purāṇa.*** II. p. 583-585.
80. ***The Yoga of Delight, Wonder and Astonishment.*** p. xxi.
81. *sa ca saṁrambho vimarśaḥ kriyāśaktir bhavati.*
Īśvara Pratyabhijñā Vimarśinī. I. p. 74.
82. *bhāvān ābhāsayan kartā nirmale svātmadarpaṇe I kāryakāraṇabhāvaṁ ca yaś citraṁ taṁ stumaḥ śivam II*
Īśvara Pratyabhijñā Vimarśinī. II. p. 150.
83. *vikalpa eva sa parapratiyogyav abhāsajaḥ.*
Īśvara Pratyabhijñā Vimarśinī. I p. 313.
84. *śaktiḥ śivasya śivatā śakteḥ śiva eva cāsti śaktitvam.*
Svātantryadarpaṇa. p. 32.
85. *jñānaṁ sadāśivatve kriyeśvaratve avabhātyabhinnāpi. ubhayatra vartamānā śaktir devasya śuddhavidyākhyā.*
Svātantryadarpaṇa. pp. 32-33.
86. *māyāśaktiḥ paramā śambhor bhedāvabhāsanonmukhatā.*
Svātantryadarpaṇa. p. 34.
87. *bhedaḥ kathaṁ nu pūrne bhāti.*
Svātantryadarpaṇa. p. 43.
88. *bandho mokṣaḥ śivasya śivateyam. advaita-mātra-rūpo yāyād dvaitaṁ kathaṁ nu suvicitram*
Svātantryadarpaṇa. pp. 47-49.
89. *pañcavidhatvaṁ śāstre, māhaiśvaryasya sammataṁ śaive I sṛṣṭi-sthiti-*

saṁhārā, apidhānam anugrahaśca tadbhedāḥ II
Svātantryadarpaṇa. p. 51.

90. Kramrisch vividly describes the *āliṅgana* of Śiva thus: Her right arm relaxedly rests on Śiva's thigh while her face turns slightly towards her solemn preceptor, whose main left arm embraces her, letting the hand touch her breast... Her sweetly serene face, suffused with sensuality, conveys the pleasure that Śiva's hand causes by holding her breast... Śiva's large, main left hand encircling Pārvatī's breast, while his main right hand is raised in the gesture giving silent exposition, *vyākhyānamudrā.* Kramrisch, Stella, ***Manifestations of Śiva***, Philadelphia Museum of Art, 1981. pp. 128-130.
91. ***The Doctrine of Vibration.*** p. 48.
92. ***The Doctrine of Vibration.*** p. 107.
93. *yathā vahnirudodhito dāhyam dahati tathā viśayapāśān bhakṣayet.*
    Pratyabhijñāhrdayam. p. 90.
94. *paripūrṇāni śūddhāni bhaktimanti sthirāṇi ca.*
    Śivastotrāvalī. 17.43
95. *tathā hi yadā yadā bahirmukham rūpam svarūpe viśrāmyati tadā tadā bāhya-vastūpasaṁhāraḥ.*
    Pratyabhijñāhṛdayam. pp. 69-70.
96. *visvottīrṇam viśvamayaṁ ca.*
    Pratybhijñāhṛdayam. p. 68.
97. ***Kumārasaṁbhava*** 7.1
98. *sarvopamā dravyasamuccayena yathāpradeśaṁ viniveśitena I sā nirmitā viśvasṛjā praytnādekasthasaundaryadidṛkṣyeva II*
    Kumārasaṁbhava 1.49
99. ***Saundaryalaharī*** of Śaṅkarācārya. V.K.Subramanian (editor). verses 43-100.
100. ***Śiva-Purāṇa.*** Volume 2. 10-17, p. 711.
101. ***Rasamañjarī.*** verse 67.
102. ***Kumārasambhava.*** Canto 8.
103. *ta ātmopāsakāḥ śaivaṁ na gacchanti param padam.*
     Pratyabhijñāhṛdayam. p. 69.
104. *caitanyātmanaḥ svarūpāt uditasya asya viśvasya bhūyaḥ punaḥ vigalitbhedasaṁskārātmanā bāhulyena ca pratimīlanam.*
     Śiva Sūtras. p. 230.
105. *bhittvā dvaitamahāmoham.*
     Śiva Sutras. p. 205.
106. *ekam ekasvabhāvatvāt jñānaṁ jñeyaṁ vibhāvyate.*
     The Yoga of Delight, Wonder and Astonishment. p. 127.
107. *rudra-yāmala-tantrasya sāram . . . hṛdayam jñātam adya ca.*
     The Yoga of Delight. Wonder and Astonishment. p. 146.
108. ***The Doctrine of Vibration.*** p. 141.
109. ***The Doctrine of Vibration.*** p. 109

110. ***The Doctrine of Vibration.*** p. 105.
111. *prakāśāvasthitaṁ jñānaṁ bhavābhāvādimadhyataḥ.*
The Yoga of Delight, Wonder and Astonishment. p. 59.
The *sūtra* appears originally in ***Tantrāloka***, verse 84.
112. *bhāve tyakte niruddhā cin naiva bhāvāntaraṁ vrajet* / *tadā tanmadhyabhāvena vikasatyatibhāvanā* //
Vijñānabhairava. 62.
113. ***The Doctrine of Vibration.*** p. 101.
114. *kriyātaḥ svātmabodhosti vibudhaiḥ kathyate sadā* / *paripūrṇasvātmabodhaḥ praśāntiṁ samprayacchati* //
Śivapārvatīvivāha. 4 (see appendix)
115. *antarmukhe saṁvidātmani proktanayena kaḥ kālaḥ.*
Parātrīśikā Vivaraṇa. p. 56 (text)
116. *kevaṁ khalu bhāṣā.*
ibid.
117. *śirīṣa-kusuma-pallava-śatavyatibheda iva yugapat iti.*
ibid.
118. *didṛkṣayeva sarvārthān yadā vyapyāvatiṣṭhate* / *tada kim bahu-noktena svayam evāvabhotsyate* //
Spandakārikā, 3.11; ***Śiva Sūtras***. p. 76.
119. *cakreśatvasiddhiḥ.*
Śiva Sūtras. p. 75.
120. *śuddhavidyodayāc cakreśatvasiddhiḥ.*
Śiva Sūtras. p. 75.
121. *tasmāt sā tu parā vidyā yasmāt anyā na vidyāte.*
Śiva Sūtras. p. 75.
122. Tagore, Rabindranath
Sādhanā, The Realization of Life, p. 97.
123. *yatra yatra manastuṣṭir manas tatraiva dhārayet* / *tatra tatra parānandasvarupaṁ saṁpravartate* //
Vijñānabhairava. 74.
124. ***The Doctrine of Vibration.*** p. 80.
125. *vismayo yogabhumikāḥ.*
Śiva Sūtras. p. 51.
126. ***The Doctrine of Vibration.*** p. 100.
127. ***The Aphorisms of Śiva***. p. 3.
128. *kuhanena prayogeṇa sadya eva mṛgekṣaṇe* / *samudeti mahanando yena tattvaṁ prakāśate* //
Vijñānabhairava. 66.
129. *ahaṁ-pratyavamarśo yaḥ prakāśātmāpi vagvapuḥ.*
Īśvara Pratyabhijñā Vimarśinī. I. p. 302.
130. *tatra śuddho yaḥ saṁvinmātre viśvābhinne viśvacchāyāc curit ācchātmani vā.*
Īśvara Pratyabhijñā Vimarśinī. I. p. 313.

131. ***Śvetāśvatara Upaniṣad.*** 2.14
132. ***Taittirīya Upaniṣad.*** 2.7
133. *atikruddhaḥ prahṛṣṭo vā kiṁ karomi iti vā mṛśan.*
The Yoga of Vibration and Divine Pulsation. 1.22
134. *kutūhale kṣudhādyante brahmasattamayī daśā.*
Vijñānabhairava. 118
135. *ānande mahati prāpte dṛṣṭe vā bāndhave cirāt.*
Vijñānabhairava. 71.
136. ***Yogasūtras.*** 1
137. *yoginaś cakṣurādīni indriyāṇi hi saṁsāranāt yaprakaṭana-pramodanirbharaṁ svasvarūpam antarmukhatayā sākṣātkurvanti, tat-prayoga-prarūḍhyā vigalityibhāgāṁ camtkārarasa-saṁpūrṇatām āpādayanti.*
Śiva Sūtras. p. 156.
138. *vismayo yogabhūmikāḥ.*
Śiva Sūtras. p. 51.
139. *ātmā caivātmanā jñāto yadā bhavati sadhakaiḥ, tadā vismayamātmā vai ātmanyaiva prapaśyati.*
Śiva Sūtras. p. 51.
140. *yathā sātiśayavastudarśane kasyacit vismayo bhavati tathā asya mahāyogino nityam tat-advedyāvabhāsāmarśābhogeṣu niḥsāmānyātiśaya-nava-nava-camatkāra-cidghanasvātmāveśavaśāt smera-smera-stimita-vikasita-samasta-karaṇa-cakrasaya yo vismay anavacinnānande svātmani aparitṛptatvena muhur muhur āścaryāyamāṇatā tā eva yogasya paratattvaikyasya saṁbandhinyo bhūmikāḥ tad-adhyāroha-viśrāntisūcikāh parimitā bhūmayo na tu kanda bindu-ādyanubhava-vṛttayaḥ.*
Śiva Sūtras. p. 51.
141. *asphuṭatvāt bhūtamiva artham abhūtamiva sphuṭvāpadanena bhāvyate yayā.*
quoted by Jaideva Singh in ***Śiva Sūtras***. p. xxxiii.
142. ***The Aphorisms of Śiva***. p. 198.
143. *nānāvidha-varṇānām rūpaṁ dhatte yathāmalaḥ sphaṭikaḥ.*
Paramārthasāra. 6.
144. *darpaṇa-bimbe yadvan nagara-grāmādi-citraṁ vibhāgī, bhāti vibhāge naiva ca parasparam darpaṇād api ca.*
Paramārthasāra. 12.
145. *dṛśyam śarīram.*
Śiva Sūtras. 1.14
146. *viśrāntirūpa akulasattā-āsādane bhairavatā.*
Parātrīśikā Vivaraṇa. p. 102 (text).
147. ***The Doctrine of Vibration.*** p. 79.
148. *evam etāsvavasthāsūktayuktyā prathamaṁ spandaśaktiṁ pariśīlya.*
The Yoga of Vibration and Divine Pulsation. introduction to 1.23-25.
149. *yāgotra parameśāni tuṣṭir ānandalakṣaṇā . . . bhāvanā parā.*
The Yoga of Delight, Wonder and Astonishment. p. 138.
150. *bhūyo bhūyaḥ pare bhāve bhāvanā bhāvyate hi yā.*

The Yoga of Delight, Wonder and Astonishment. p. 133.
151. ***Parātrīśika Vivaraṇa.*** p. 37.
152. *bhāvanā mantra nyāsa-homādi-rūp kāñcid eva siddhiṁ vitaret.*
Parātrīśikā Vivaraṇa. p. 53 (text).
153. ***The Presence of Śiva.*** p. 428.
154. *svarūpa-bahurūpāya namaḥ saṁvinmayāya te.*
Śivastotrāvalī. 2.1
155. *jaḍe jagati cidrūpaḥ.*
Śivastotrāvali. 3.20
156. ***Śiva Purāṇa.*** p. 576.
157. ***Śiva Purāṇa.*** p. 576.
158. ***Śiva Purāṇa.*** p. 577.
159. ***The Presence of Śiva.*** p. 357.
160. ***Śiva Purāṇa.*** p.584.
161. ***Śiva Purāṇa.*** p.586.
162. ***Śiva Purāṇa.*** p.676.
163. ***Śiva Purāṇa.*** p. 677.
164. ***Śiva Purāṇa.*** p. 587.
165. *śrotrasya śrotram, manaso mano yad vāco ha vācam sa u prāṇasya prāṇaḥ.* ***Kenopaniṣad.*** 2
166. ***Kaṭha Upaniṣad*** 2.6 10-11.
167. ***Chāndogya Upaniṣad.*** 6.12
in ***The Thirteen Principal Upaniṣads.*** p. 248.
168. ***The Doctrine of Vibration.*** p. 71.
169. ***The Doctrine of Vibration.*** p. 70.
170. *viśvarūpo aham idam.*
Īśvara Pratyabhijñā Vimarśinī. II. p. 280.
171. ***The Doctrine of Vibration.*** p. 69.
172. *śuddhatattva-sandhānād vā apaśuśaktiḥ.*
Śiva Sūtras. p. 61.
173. *paśvākhyā bandhaśaktiḥ.*
Śiva Sūtras. p. 62.
174. ***The Aphorisms of Śiva.*** p. 47.
175. *sarvaṁ dehaṁ cinmayaṁ hi jagadvā paribhāvayet / yugapan nirvikalpena manasā paramodbhavaḥ //*
Śiva Sūtras. p. 62.
176. *viśvātmā śiva evāsmi iti yo vitarko vicāraḥ.*
Śiva Sūtras. p. 64
177. *svarūpā-bhedātmka-bindusvarūpadvāreṇa anuttarapada eva saṁkramāt svarūpa eva viśrāntiḥ.*
Paratrīśikā Vivaraṇa p. 67 (text).
178. *tasya ca pramātur antaḥ sarvārthāvabhāsaḥ.*
Īśvara Pratyabhijñā Vimarśinī. I. p. 309.
179. *samānādhikaraṇyañca sadvidyā-aham-idaṁ-dhiyoḥ.*
Īśvara Pratyabhijñā Vimarśinī. II. p. 221.

180. ***The Aphorisms of Śiva.*** pp. 68-69.
181. *mantrāṇām rahasyam.*
Śiva Sūtras. p. 89.
182. ***Muṇḍaka Upaniṣad*** 2.2.3-4.
quoted by Dyczkowski in ***The Aphorisms of Śiva.*** p. 199.
183. *jāgradādivibhedepi tadabhinne prasarpati / nivartate nijānnaiva svabhāvād upalabdhṛtaḥ //*
The Yoga of Vibration and Divine Pulsation. p. 34.
184. *pariṇāmo acetanasya cetanasya na yujyate.*
The Yoga of Vibration and Divine Pulsation. p. 35.
185. *sa śaṅkara evetyupadiṣṭam bhavati.*
The Yoga of Vibration and Divine Pulsation. p. 35.
186. *avasthāsyeva bhedo'yam nāvasthātuḥ kadācana / yathā viṣasyāṅ kurādau tad śakterna tu bhinnatā //*
The Yoga of Vibration and Divine Pulsation. p. 39.
187. *mātureva tad-anyonyāviyukte jñānakarmaṇi.*
Īśvara Pratyabhijñā Vimarśinī. II. p. 214.
188. *śrīmat-sadāśivodāra-prārambhaṁ vasudhāntakam / yadantarbhāti tattvānām cakraṁ taṁ saṁstumaḥ śivam //*
Īśvara Pratyabhijñā Vimarśinī. II. p. 211.
189. *iti tad-anusāreṇa padārtha-nirṇayam viśva-prameyīkaraṇa-pratilabdhatadviśvottīrṇa pramātṛpada-hṛdayaṅgamīkāra-abhiprāyeṇa nirūpayitum.*
Īśvara Pratyabhijñā Vimarśinī. II. p. 213.
190. *tad anyonya-aviyukte jñānakarmaṇī.*
Īśvara Pratyabhijñā Vimarśinī. II. p. 2.
191. *tasmād aviyuktam jñānaṁ kriyā ca. jñānaṁ vimarśānuprāṇitam, vimarśa eva ca kriyeti.*
Īśvara Pratyabhijñā Vimarśinī. II. p. 215.
192. *yadyapi ekam eva śivatattvaṁ tadīyam eva svātantryaṁ svātmani svarūpabhedaṁ tāvat pratibimba-kalpayatā darśayati.*
Īśvara Pratyabhijñā Vimarśinī. II. p. 217.
193. *tatraivaṁ svātmani maheśvare sthite tasmin eva prakāśarūpe svātmadarpaṇe tenaiva parameśvareṇa svātantryāt tāvat sṛṣṭaḥ sañkoca-puraḥsara idaṁ-bhāgaḥ.*
Īśvara Pratyabhijñā Vimarśinī. II p. 282.
194. *akhaṇḍita-svabhāvopi vicitrāṁ mātṛkalpanām.*
Īśvara Pratyabhijñā Vimarśinī. II. p. 243.
195. *yatra sthitam idaṁ sarvaṁ kāryam yasmācca nirgatam.*
The Yoga of Vibration and Divine Pulsation. p. 24.
196. *na tu yo'antarmukho bhāvaḥ sarvajñatvaguṇāspadam.*
The Yoga of Vibration and Divine Pulsation. p. 80.
197. *yathā nyagrodhabījasthaḥ śaktirūpo mahādrumaḥ / tathā hṛdayabījasthaṁ jagadetaccarācaram //*
The Yoga of Vibration and Divine Pulsation. p. 25.

198. *paramārtha parameśvara sarvato viviktaḥ paramakāraṇam parātmā ayam aham asmi iti pratipadyeta.*
The Yoga of Vibration and Divine Pulsation. p. 5.

199. *na hi tasya śabdādivad idantayā svarūpam upalakṣayitum śakyam.*
The Yoga of Vibration and Divine Pulsation. p. 5.

200. *iti vā yasya saṁvittiḥ krīḍātvenākhilaṁ jagat.*
The Yoga of Vibration and Divine Pulsation. p. 119.

Bibliography

PRIMARY SOURCES

The Aphorisms of Śiva. The Śiva Sūtra with Bhāskara's Commentary, the Vārttika. Dyczkowski, M.S.G. (translator), State University of New York Press. Albany. 1992.

Ātmabodha. Śaṅkarācārya.

Īśvara Pratyabhijñā Vimarśinī. Doctrine of Divine Recognition. Pandey, K.C. (translator). Volume I, II and III. Motilal Banarsidass. Delhi. 1954.

Kāvyaprakāśa, Mammaṭa. Dwivedi, R.C. (editor). Motilal Banarsidass. Delhi. 1986.

Kulārṇava Tantra. Rai, Ram Kumar (editor). Prachya Prakashan. Varanasi. 1983.

Kumārasaṁbhava. Kālidāsa.

Paramārthasāra. Essence of the Exact Reality. Pandit, B.N. (translator). Munshiram Manoharlal. Delhi. 1991.

Parātrīśikā Vivaraṇa of Abhinavagupta. Singh, Jaideva (translator), Baümer, Bettina (editor). Motilal Banarsidass, Delhi. 1988.

Pratybhijñāhṛdayam. The Secret of Self-recognition. Singh, Jaideva (translator). Motilal Banarsidass. Delhi. 1963.

Saundaryalaharī. Śaṅkarācārya. Subramanian. V.K. (translator). Motilal Banarsidass. Delhi. 1977.

Śiva Purāṇa. Ancient Indian Tradition and Mythology Series. Volumes I, II, III and IV. Motilal Banarsidass. Delhi. 1970.

Śivastotrāvalī of Utpaladeva. Shaiva Devotional Songs of Kāśmīr. Bailly, C.R. (translator). State University of New York Press.

Albany. 1987.

Śiva Sūtras. The Yoga of Supreme Identity. Singh, Jaideva (translator). Motilal Banarsidass. Delhi. 1979.

Svātantryadarpaṇaḥ. The Mirror of Self Supremacy. Pandit, B.N. (translator). Munshiram Manoharlal. Delhi. 1993.

Vijñānabhairava or Divine Consciousness. Singh, Jaideva (translator) Motilal Banarsidass. Delhi. 1979.

The Yoga of Delight, Wonder and Astonishment. A Translation of the Vijñānabhairava. Singh, Jaideva (translator). State University of New York Press. Albany. 1991.

The Yoga of Vibration and Divine Pulsation. A Translation of the Spandakārikās with Kṣemarāja's Commentary, the Spanda-Nirnaya, Singh, Jaideva (translator). State University of New York Press. Albany. 1992.

Yogasūtra. Patañjali.

SECONDARY SOURCES

Abhinavagupta: An Historical and Philosophical Study. Pandey, K.C. Chowkhamba Sanskrit Office. Varanasi. 1963.

The Advaita of Art. Dehejia, Harsha V. Motilal Banarsidass, Delhi. 1995.

Another Harmony. Blackburn, Stuart H. and Ramanujan, A. K. (editors). Oxford University Press, Delhi, 1986.

Basholi Paintings of the Rasamañjarī. Randhawa and Bhambri. Humanities Press, Atlantic Highlands. N.J., 1981.

The Development of Hindu Iconography. Banerjea, Jitendra Nath. University of Calcutta, Calcutta. 1956.

The Doctrine of Vibration. An Analysis of the Doctrines and Practices of Kāśmīr Śaivism. Dyczkowski, M.S.G. State University of New York Press. Albany. 1987.

History of the Tantric Religion. Bhattacharya, N.N. Manohar Publications. New Delhi. 1982.

The Hour of God and Other Writings. Aurobindo, Sri. Volume 17. Centenary Edition. Sri Aurobindo Birth Centenary Library, Pondicherry, 1971.

Indian Idealism. Dasgupta, Surendranath. University Press. Cambridge. 1962.

Indian Philosophy. Radhakrishnan, S. Volume 1 and 2. George, Allen and Unwin Ltd., London. 1923.

The Mythic Image. Campbell, Joseph. Princeton University Press. Princeton. 1974.

Nepal Where The Gods Are Young. Pal, Pratapadiya. The Asia Society New York. 1975.

The Sacred Marriage of a Hindu Goddess. Harman, William P. Motilal Banarsidass, Delhi, 1989.

Sādhanā. The Realization of Life, Rabindranath Tagore, Omen Communication Inc., 1972.

Śakti and Śākta. Woodroffe, Sir John. Ganesh & Co. (Madras) Private Ltd., Madras, 1959.

Significance of the Tantric Tradition. Mishra, Kamlakar. Arddhanarisvara Publications, Varanasi, 1981.

Tantra, The Indian Cult of Ecstasy. Philip Rawson. Thomas and Hudson, London, 1973.

Tapasvinī Pārvatī. Joshi, N.P. New Age International Limited, Publishers. New Delhi. 1996.

The Thirteen Principal Upanishads. Hume, Robert Ernest. Oxford University Press. London, 1975.

The Triadic Heart of Śiva. Muller-Ortega, P.E. State University of New York Press. Albany, 1989.

Vaiṣṇava Iconography in the Tamil Country. Champakalakshmi, R. Orient Longman, New Delhi, 1981.

Women, Androgynes and other Mythical Beasts. O'Flaherty, Wendy. The University of Chicago Press, Chicago, 1988.

Glossary

A.

A. The first letter of the alphabet. It is the one letter that pervades all other letters of the alphabet and is therefore considered the manifestation of Śiva.

Anusandhāna. repeated intensive awareness, an awareness that implies synthesis. The Kāśmīr Śaivites use the term *pratyabhijñā* to express a similar idea.

Aham. meaning "I am". It is considered the first step in a three step cognition that leads to self-awareness. It is also sometimes called *ahantā.*

Ānanda. bliss

Ānandatāṇḍava. Śiva's dance of bliss.

Advaita. non-dual. It refers to the concept that man and God are ultimately one. Śaṅkara was the first to systematise the concept of *advaiṭa* into a philosophic system. The Kāśmīr Śaivite *advaita* is a richer and affirmative system.

Āgama. Old or ancient or traditional. The *āgamas* are considered the traditional and pre-historic scriptures of the Indian tradition. Although they accept the authority of the Vedas they exposit a world-view different from that of the *nigamas.*

Āgamavāda. The system that exposits the Āgamic viewpoint.

Āgamācārya. A master or *guru* that teaches the Āgamic system.

Artha. Meaning.

Ādivāsī. The aboriginal people of India.

Abhidhā. The primary or the expressed meaning of the word.

Anirvacanīya. unexplainable, mysterious.

Ardhanārīśvara. The androgyn image of Śiva and Pārvatī as half man and half woman.

Āsīdekam. primal voidness.

Ādināṭya. the first drama as described in the ***Nāṭyaśāstra***.

Ābhāsa. reflection. In Kāśmīr Śaivism it refers to the objective world as a reflection of Śiva.

Apohana. the epistemic process of knowledge by negation.

Āliṅgana. embrace.

Apidhānam. conceal.

Anugraha. support, follow.

Ātman. the microcosmic or individual reality.

Adbhuta. wonder.

Anusvāra. nasal sound indicated by a dot.

Antarmukho. inwards, introspective.

E.

Ekarasa. unitary state of consciousness.

I.

Icchā. desire or will. One of the three features of Śiva the others being *jñāna* and *kriyā*.

Indriya. sense-organ. The Indian tradition regards the mind as the sixth sense-organ besides the usual five, viz. touch, smell, taste, hearing and sight.

Idam. meaning this, it refers to the objective as opposed to the subjective.

Īkṣita. seeing, beholding, visual perception. Kāśmīr Śaivite epistemology gives pride of place to this form of perception.

U.

Unmeṣa. also *unmīlana,* literally meaning opening of the eyes. In Kāśmīr Śaivism it refers to the cognition of the objective world.

***Unmīlana samādhi*:** a state of mind in which the eyes are open and the external world appears as universal consciousness or Śiva.

Upeya. to be striven after.

Upāya. means or expedient.

K.

Kriyā. activity, especially creative epistemic activity.

Karuṇā. compassion. The Buddhists made this an important concept in their plank.

Kinnara. Mythic musicians that take the form of half man and half animal.

Kāvya. poetry.

Kāmadhenu. the wish-fulfilling cow.

Kartṛtva. the state of being the doer.

G.

Ghūrṇana. subtle stress or vibration.

C.

Cit. Absolute foundational consciousness.

Citta. individual consciousness.

Cittavṛtti. the activity of consciousness.

Citra. painting.

Cintāmaṇi. the mythic wish-fulfilling jewel.

Cidānanda. blissful consciousness.

Cidānandaghana. mass of blissful consciousness.

J.

Jñāna. refers to *brahma-jñāna* or spiritual knowledge.

Jarjara. The pole or staff of Indra that is ceremonially planted on the stage at the commencement of a dramatic performance.

Jagadānanda. The ability of deriving a blissful experience from the common world.

Jāgrata. one who is awake. Vedānta uses the metaphor of states of awakening to levels of knowledge.

Jaḍa. the inconscient matter.

T.

Trika. Kāśmīr Śaivism is also sometimes called the Trika philosophy because it emphasises the trinity of *jñāna*, *icchā* and *kriyā*.

Tapas. heat, radiance, internal spiritual effort. The Vedic concept of *yajña* was transformed in the Upaniṣads to that of *tapas*.

Tantra. a manual of instructions. Sometimes the term is used synonymously with *Āgama*.

Trikāla. the past, present and future.

Trikālabādhyam. bound by the three-fold time.

Tanmayī-bhāva. state of detachment as prescribed by the *rasa* doctrine as preparation for a perfect *rasa* experience

Tuṣṭi. pleasure, happiness, satisfaction.

Tāṇḍava. Śiva's dance.

Tadbhinna. different from.

D.

Dhāraṇā. concentration.

Darśana. vision, insight. It refers either to the schools of philosophy or the interaction between a devotee and the icon.

Deśī. the folk or the indigenous.

Dvaita. dualism of man and God and subject and object.

Dhvani. reverberation. A type of extended metaphor.

Darpaṇa. mirror.

Dhyāna. concentration.

Ḍ.

Ḍamarū. a drum. Held by Śiva in his right hand it is the symbol of the first sound or *praṇava* that led to creation.

N.

Nimeṣa. literally meaning closing of the eyelids or dissolution of the world. It refers to the inner activity of *spanda* by which the object is merged into the subject.

Nirvikalpa. devoid of thought constructs, non-conceptual.

Nirvāṇa. Buddhist term for ultimate spiritual freedom.

Nyagrodha. The banyan or the Indian fig tree. The *Bhagvad-Gītā* in chapter 15 describes life as an upside down banyan tree.

Nirguṇa. without attributes.

Nigama. the scriptures of the Vedic and *vedāntic* stream.

Nāyaka. Hero.

Nāyikā. Heroine.

Nandī. Śiva's favourite bull and his mount.

Nirodha. cessation.

Nyāsa. putting down, placing, fixing, inserting, organising.

Nirānanda. devoid of bliss.

P.

Prakāśa. literally meaning light, it refers to pure consciousness. While the *advaita vedāntins* postulate *brahman* as just *prakāśa* the Kāśmīr Śaivites claim that *brahman* is not just *prakāśa* but *prakāśa-vimarśamaya.*

Pramā. knowledge.

Pramāṇa. means of knowledge.

Pramātṛ. subject of knowledge or knower.

Prameya. object of knowledge or what is to be known.

Pratibhā. creative consciousness.

Pratimīlana. a combination of *unmīlana* and *nimīlana* or the experience of divinity both within and outside.

Pratibimba. reflection of a reflection.

Pratyabhijñā. cognition through recognition.

Purāṇa. ancient or mythic stories.

Parāvṛtti. turning back around.

Pūjā. worship. While *yajña* was the basic Vedic activity, *pūjā* is the basic *āgamic* religious idiom of worship.

Parokṣa. indirect, hidden or suggested. *Parokṣārtha* refers to a deeper and indirect meaning.

Pūrṇa. full, perfect.

Prajāpati. lord of creation.

Pratītyasamutpāda. the Buddhist concept of causation which asserts that one thing leads to another.

Parabrahman. The transcendent *brahman.*

Prabuddha. aroused, awakened, enlightened.

Paramaśiva. the transcendent Śiva.

Pariṇāma. transformation.

B.

Bindu. (also *Vindu*) The compact mass of consciousness gathered into an undifferentiated point ready to create.

Baindavī kalā. that power or freedom of Parama-Śiva by which the knower always remains as the knower and is never reduced to the known.

Bhāvanā. creative contemplation leading to a state where one views the object and the subject as not different from Śiva.

Bhairava. another name of Śiva; a term commonly used by Kāśmīr Śaivites in place of *brahman* to denote ultimate reality. Etymologically the term *bhairava* is derived from *bha* indicating *bharaṇa* or maintenance, *ra* from *ravana* or withdrawal of the world, and *va* or *vamana* or projection of the world.

Bhoga. literally meaning the relish of food it refers to the act of exulting in the cognition of the objective world.

Brahman. ulitmate reality. Used especially in the Upaniṣads it refers to an epistemic reality, of ultimate knowledge that needs no verification and is not contradicted. This ultimate knowledge is therefore also called *brahma-jñāna* and the seeker of that knowledge *brahma-jījñāsu.*

Brahmānanda. The state of bliss on acquiring the knowledge of *brahman.*

Bhakti. worship to a personal God. While the origins of *bhakti* are undetermined, as a cult it came into prominence in mediaeval India.

Bimba. reflection. It carries the same connotation as *ābhāsa.*

Bhedābheda. unity in difference. The same meaning is conveyed by the term *śiva-śakti-sāmarasya.*

Bhakṣayet. to consume with relish.

Badhra. a weapon. The term is applied to the attribute or weapon that a mythic figure carries.

Bhāva. emotion.

Bṛhat. vast.

M.

Manas. the emotive mind that is considered the sixth sense-organ since it works closely with other senses in building perceptions and inferences.

Mantra. a sacred word or formula to be chanted. Etymologically derived from *manana* or reflection and *trāṇa* or protection. In Kāśmīr Śaivism the *citta* itself becomes *mantra.*

Mantroccāra. the utterance of a *mantra.*

Māyā. the term carries several meanings. Epistemically in Śaṅkara's Advaita Vedānta it means the unexplainable illusion of the world. In Kāśmīr Śaivism, however, it refers to the power and freedom of the infinite to concretise itself in the finite.

Madanikā. sensuous female.

Mārgī. the high road or the classical, as opposed to the folk.

Mahākāvya. an epic poem. A *mahākāvya* had to follow many conventions one of which was that it should have a happy ending.

Maṇḍapa. a hall. Usually a part of the temple and called variously as *kalyāṇa-maṇḍapa* or *raṅga-maṇḍapa* or *sabhā-maṇḍapa.*

Maṇḍala. mystic diagram.

Mithuna. a couple in sexual bliss. A visual paradigm of perfect knowledge in Kāśmīr Śaivism signifying the coming together of the subject and the object in perfect harmony and in a state of ecstasy.

Madhya-bhāva. an intermediate epistemic stage as between waking and dreaming.

Mūlādhāra. one of the seven *cakras* situated above the generative organs.

Mithyā. false or illusory.

Y.

Yoga. literally meaning to join, it refers to a variety of practices by which the mind is stilled and led into a transcendent state.

Yogī, Yoginī. one who is adept in *yoga.*

Yajña. sacrifice, referring to the Vedic fire sacrifice.

Yakṣī. celestial female commonly depicted as a sensuous female touching a tree with her left foot and bringing it to blossom.

Yamala. couple.

R.

Raṅga-maṇḍapa. the theatre of the temple which is usually situated between the entrance and the sanctum of the temple.

Rasa. aesthetic emotion. There are nine traditional *rasas*.

Rasānanda. The bliss of a *rasa* experience.

Rasabrahman. The state of bliss arrived by a *rasa* experience.

Rūpa. aesthetic form.

Rūpabrahman. The state of bliss arrived at by a *rūpa* experience.

Ṛṣi. sage or seer.

L.

Lakṣaṇā. metaphor.

V.

Vāmā. literally meaning to emit, it refers to a married woman who stands to the left of her husband. In the Śiva-Pārvatī myth it obviously refers to Pārvatī.

Vikalpa. a specific thought construct.

Vidyā. knowledge.

Vimarśa. that aspect of consciousness that creates and cognises the objective world.

Viśrānti. rest, used mainly in the sense of epistemic rest.

Varṇāśramadharma. the traditional caste system of dividing society into four castes.

Viśiṣṭādvaita. qualified non-dualism. It refers to the *bhakti* school of philosophy systematised by Rāmānuja.

Viśeṣa-spanda. the stir or activity of consciousness. It carries the same meaning as *cittavṛtti*.

Viśvarūpa. cosmic form which contains the entire microcosm.

Vindu. same as *Bindu*.

Vivarta. uncovered.

S, Ś

Śakti. the creative aspect of consciousness synonymous with *vimarśa*. In the *Śākta* tradition it refers to the various Mother Goddesses.

Śiva. the mythic god, a part of the trinity. The term as used in Kāśmīr does not carry any theological connotations and refers to ultimate and transcendent reality.

Śūddha-vidyā. pure knowledge or knowledge which blends the objective with the subjective, Pārvatī and Śiva.

Sadvidyā. same as *śuddha-vidyā*.

Śūnya(tā). meaning void, it was developed into a system of Buddhist philosophy by Nāgārjuna.

Śraddhā. committment, faith.

Smṛti. what is remembered. It refers to all religious texts other than *śruti* including *Mahābhārata* and the *Rāmāyaṇa*.

Saguṇa. with attributes. Usually applied to ultimate reality with attributes.

Savikalpa. with thought constructs, something that can be conceptualised.

Śabda. while generically it refers to any word, specifically it refers to the Vedic word.

Sādhanā. spiritual endeavour.

Sādhaka. one who undertakes *sādhanā*.

Siddhi. skill, spiritual power.

Spanda. Spandana. vibration or pulsation or throbbing. The term is special to the Kāśmīr Śaivites who refer to the epistemic throbbing of Śiva as *spandana*. It is likened to the cyclical indrawing and outdrawing of breath.

Sphuraṇa. same as *spandana*.

Smaraṇa. remembrance. In Kāśmīr Śaivite epistemology it refers to the correction of a primal amnesia and is an important part of the epistemic process. The hero of a story forgets the heroine, but then remembers her through a sign and brings the narrative to a happy ending. Similarly Śiva has forgotten that Pārvatī is none other than Satī of a previous birth but upon repeated cognitions remembers.

Samatā. oneness, harmony.

Śleṣa. the figure of speech of using a word with multiple meanings.

Sāmarasya. oneness, harmony.

Śivatva. Śivaness or Śivahood, the essence of being Śiva.

Śivarātri. The 13th day of Māgha observed traditionally as the day Śiva and Pārvatī got married.

Sampradāya. sect. There are three main *sampradāyas* viz. Śiva, Viṣṇu and Śakti and two minor *sampradāyas* that of Sūrya and Gaṇeśa.

Śāstra. scripture or traditional text.

Śilpa. sculpture.

Sahodara. twin brother. In Sanskrit criticism the term *brahmānanda-sahodara*, the twin brother of *brahman*, is used to denote a *rasa* experience.

Śrivāstava. the geometric form on the chest of Viṣṇu signifying Lakṣmī.

Śeṣaśāyī. Reclining on the thousand-hooded snake, Ādiśeṣa. An epithet of Viṣṇu.

Saṁskāras. rites of passage. Traditionally there are 16 such *saṁskāras* from birth to death.

Sākṣāt. direct. *Sākṣātārtha* refers to a direct, immediate or surface meaning.

Śānta. peaceful.

Śāntabrahmavāda. Another term for Śaṅkara's Advaita Vedānta where *brahman* is passive and devoid of activity.

Svāntantrya. freedom. In Kāśmīr Śaivism the term refers to the freedom of Śiva to manifest himself as the objective world.

Suṣupta. deep sleep. Epistemically it refers to the state of *nirvikalpa jñāna* or perfect knowledge in the Upaniṣads and Advaita Vedānta in particular.

Suṣumnā. the state of deep sleep. The term is used generally in its epistemic sense indicating *nirvikalpa-jñāna.*

Samādhi. the state of holding the mind in perfect equilibrium.

Sūtra. thread, lines of a didactic verse.

Sṛṣṭi. creation

Sthiti. maintenance.

Saṁhāra. reabsorption. This should not be understood as death but as returning to the source as a river enters the ocean.

Śṛṅgāra. romantic.

Sādhāraṇīkaraṇa. universalisation. The term is used in the *rasa* doctrine to denote the process of converting the particular into the universal.

Saṁkalpa. determination.

Saṁskāra. latent psychic impression.

Saṁvega. shock or wonder.

Satyam. what is true.

Svapna. dream.

H.

Homa. sacrificial offering.